GOOD NEWS

IN

ISRAEL'S FEASTS

#3 The One New Man Series

by
Paul & Nuala O'Higgins

Published by Reconciliation Outreach Inc

P.O. Box 2778, Stuart, Florida 34995

Printed by ACTSCo. Ltd.

Chiang Mai, Thailand

www.actsco.org

CONTENTS

INTRODUCTION

The Feasts of the Lord are a blueprint of God's great redemptive plan. He is at work to bring mankind from slavery and hopelessness to full participation in His own life and nature.

The seven feasts, which we shall examine in this book, contain an extraordinary pattern prefiguring the redemptive work of the Messiah Jesus.

Like the Feasts of the Lord the redemptive work of Jesus takes place in two major seasons. The Spring Festivals anticipate the redemptive works of His crucifixion and resurrection. The Fall Feasts anticipate the climactic events of the end of the age when Jesus will return to complete the redemption of the world and of His followers. Between the two seasons is the Feast of Pentecost, which illustrates

5

the sustaining presence of the Spirit of God who keeps, guides and matures the people of God until the end of the age.

White light when passed through a prism is broken into a rainbow of brilliant colors. So too the—Feasts of the Lord provide a prism which divide the work of redemption into seven parts to better enable us to understand and enter into the awesome plan of God

1) in Israel's history,
2) in the redemption of the world and
3) in the spiritual journey of the believer as the Spirit leads him from glory to glory.

"And we all, with unveiled face, beholding the glory of the Lord, are being changed into his likeness from one degree of glory to another; for this comes from the Lord who is the Spirit." (2 Cor. 3:18)

The Feasts illustrate the dynamic and progressive nature of the life of faith. This life of faith is not a stagnant thing which begins and ends

6

with the appropriation of the gift of forgiveness, but a process of transformation from dimension to dimension, from glory to glory and from grace to grace.

A study of these Feasts in the light of the work of redemption can enrich and expand our understanding of the glories of the gospel. They can help us to see the plan of God for individuals and for the world as a dynamic unfolding of His mercy in time. Finally they can challenge us to aspire for higher and higher levels of spiritual living.

This book focuses on the Feasts of the Lord as they illustrate the redemptive work of the Lord in the plan of history and in the life of the individual believer. We have not, in the limited confines of this short work, focused on the details of all of the symbols and rituals associated with each feast.

Our prayer is that all who read this book will be inspired to lay hold of the call of God on their lives, follow Him more closely than ever before and be

encouraged to anticipate eagerly the good things
that are coming to the earth.

CHAPTER 1

AN OVERVIEW OF THE FEASTS

'These are the feasts of the Lord, holy convocations, which you shall proclaim at their appointed time.' 'On the fourteenth day of the first month at twilight is the Lord's **Passover***' 'And on the fifteenth day of the same month is the Feast of* **Unleavened Bread** *to the Lord; seven days you must eat unleavened bread.'*

When you come into the land, which I give to you and reap its harvest, then you, shall bring a sheaf of the **first fruits** *of your harvest to the priest. 'He shall wave the sheaf before the Lord to be accepted on your behalf.*

9

*'And you shall count for yourselves from the day after the Sabbath from the day that you brought the sheaf of the wave offering: seven **weeks** shall be completed. Count fifty days to the day after the seventh Sabbath you shall offer a new grain offering to the Lord...*

*'Then the Lord spoke to Moses, saying, 'Speak to the children of Israel, saying: 'In the seventh month, on the first day of the month, you shall have a Sabbath rest, a memorial of blowing of **trumpets**, a holy convocation. You shall do no customary work on it; and you shall offer an offering made by fire to the Lord.*

*Also the tenth day of this seventh month shall be the **Day of Atonement**. It shall be a holy convocation for you; you shall afflict your souls and offer an offering made by fire to the Lord. 'And you shall do no work on that same day, for it is the Day of Atonement, to make atonement for you before the Lord your God. 'For any person who is not afflicted in soul on that day, that person I will destroy from among his people.'*

10

"The fifteenth day of the seventh month shall be the Feast of Tabernacles for seven days to the Lord...

'And you shall take for yourselves on the first day the fruit of beautiful trees, branches of palm trees, the boughs of leafy trees and willows of the brook; and you shall rejoice before the Lord your God for seven days." (Leviticus 23)

The Feasts of the Lord were central to the Life of Israel and references to them abound throughout the scriptures both in the Old and New Testament. They contain important information concerning the plan and dimensions of our great redemption.

The seven Feasts Of The Lord Are: -

(1) Passover,

(2) Unleavened Bread,

(3) First Fruits,

(4) The Feast Of Weeks (Shavuot in Hebrew) it is also known as **"Pentecost"** (from the Greek word 'pentekoste' (meaning fiftieth) because it comes on the fiftieth day after Passover

11

(5) **The Feast of Trumpets (Yom Turah** also known as **Rosh Hashanah**)

(6) this is followed by the **Day of Atonement, (Yom Kippur)** and finally

(7) **The Feast of Tabernacles** (or Booths)
The First Three occur at the *springtime* of the year, Pentecost occurs in the *early summer* and the last three feasts are grouped together at the Fall Harvest time of the year.

Each of the feasts has a tri-fold application:

(1) they commemorate an event in the history of Israel;

(2) they point prophetically to an aspect of the redemptive work of Jesus the Messiah.

(3) they point to a stage in the subjective redemption of the believer.

The feasts commemorate great events in the history of Israel and anticipate even greater realities. As the letter to Hebrews says: *"The law has but the shadow of the good things to come instead of the true form of these realities."* (Hebrews 10:1) Paul says that the Feasts and Sabbaths are a shadow of things to come but the substance belongs to Christ. (Colossians 2; 17) And so the *feasts foreshadow even greater events* and realities than those they commemorate. They provide us with perhaps the greatest picture of the many facets of our redemption. We who come to Messiah Jesus come to the great realities anticipated by the Feasts. The Feasts & The Work of Jesus

On the way to Emmaus on the Day of His resurrection Jesus explained to two of His followers how the entire scriptures foretold His work. (Luke 24:13-30) Perhaps at that time He explained to them how His work was anticipated by the Feasts and how His life fulfilled them. The Feasts clearly illustrate the full work of Jesus. The Feasts depict seven major facets of His redemptive work, which all believers should understand.

1) **Passover** illustrates His work as the Lamb who dies for our sins so that we can be released from sins penalty.

2) **Unleavened Bread** illustrates His death for us, which brings to an end the power of sin.

3) **First Fruits** illustrates Jesus as the first born from the dead and the Head of the new creation.

4) **Pentecost** illustrates the gift of the Holy Spirit, for power.

5) **Trumpets** is the wake-up call to herald His triumphant return.

6) **Atonement** anticipates His becoming the scapegoat and bearer of all our judgments, and the judgment of the nations, which will accompany His triumphant return.

7) **Tabernacles** will be fulfilled when Jesus comes to take His place as King of the earth, to occupy the throne of David and to fill the earth with the knowledge and glory of God.

Christian Growth And The Feasts

The Feasts foreshadow and portray seven major stages of Christian growth and development:

14

1. **Passover** prefigures the covering of sin through the blood of Jesus shed on Calvary. (Rom 3:25, Eph 1:7)

2. The **Feast of Unleavened Bread** prefigures the laying aside of our old nature and life through the cross of Jesus, and the journey to our new destiny in Him (Rm. 6:3-12)

3. The **Feast of First Fruits** prefigures the receiving of the new life of the Spirit - His overcoming resurrection - life within our spirits. (John 20: 21-23)

4. The **Feast of Pentecost** commemorates the giving of The Law at Sinai and prefigures the empowerment of believers with the Holy Spirit, and the giving of the Spirit to be their guide,. (Acts 1:5)

5. **Trumpets** is a wake up call for believes that the "Bridegroom is coming", calling us to strong faith, spiritual warfare and standing with God's purposes for Israel. (Luke 21:24-31)

6. The **Day Atonement** is a further reminder that all access to God is through the remission of sins

based on the Substitution of Jesus who became our scapegoat and took our sins upon Himself. It also symbolizes the putting off of the last vestiges of sin through deeper surrender, and the refining fire of the Holy Spirit, which prepares the *"bride without spot or wrinkle"* for the return of the Bridegroom. ((Hb. 12:4-11, 1 Pt. 4)

7. **Tabernacles** anticipates the coming of the Lord to establish His kingdom outwardly on the earth and the glorification which believers will receive at His coming. (The fullness of this final state has not yet been attained by believers but is reserved for the hour of 'Yeshua's return. It also anticipates a final harvest for the Church, and the fullness of our redemption.

CHAPTER 2

THE FEAST OF PASSOVER

The first three feasts, Passover, Unleavened Bread, and First Fruits are celebrated at the Springtime of the year and commemorate the events of the Exodus when the Jewish people

(1) were rescued by the blood of the Passover Lamb,

(2) escaped Egypt and

(3) began their journey towards Canaan, the Promised Land.

The annual Passover Feast pointed back to this great event, and forward to an even greater event, which it foreshadowed - the death and resurrection

17

of Jesus. His death and resurrection is fulfills   the Passover.

Passover,

- commemorates the Exodus,

- has its objective fulfillment in Jesus' death and resurrection.

- has a personal fulfillment in each of our lives when we personally put our faith in what Jesus had done. When anyone accepts Jesus as their eternal Passover Lamb by receiving the blood of Jesus as the covering of his sins, God passes over His sins. He is then reconciled to God and God counts him as one of His children

The children Israel were spared the destruction of the Angel of Death through their faith in the blood of the Passover Lamb. In the same way we are accepted into God's Presence and emancipated from sins penalty and power when we put our faith in the Blood of Jesus, God's eternal Lamb.

18

The children of Israel were not accepted on the basis of their behavior but through their faith in the Passover Lamb. In exactly the same way we are redeemed and forgiven by putting our faith in the death of Jesus, the Lamb of God.

Each Feast was to be kept at its appointed time' (Lev. 23:4) Likewise each Feast is to be fulfilled by the Messiah at God's appointed time. Jesus kept the timetable of these feasts.

> *Passover, we are reconciled to God through Jesus' shed blood. It is finished*

Jesus, Himself was conscious of this pattern. Approximately 1500 years after the first Passover He fulfilled through His own death that which the Passover Lamb pointed to. He came in the fullness of time (Gal. 4:4). Fulfilling the pattern of the Feast of Passover His blood was shed precisely at the day and hour when the Passover lambs were killed.

He is the eternal Passover not only for the people of Israel but for all who put their faith on Him. All who apply His Blood to their lives and

19

believe that He has borne their guilt and sin are reconciled with God.

On the night of the first Passover the Children of Israel were saved from the angel of destruction when they applied the blood of the Passover Lamb to the doorposts and lintels of their houses. In exactly the same way believers who put their faith in the blood of Jesus and apply by faith the benefits of His cross to their lives receive emancipation and forgiveness. Through Him *'we have redemption through His blood the forgiveness of sin according to the riches of Hi grace'* (Ephesians 1:7)

We are delivered from the penalty of our sin, forgiven and reconciled to God through faith in the **objective fact** that the blood of the Lamb has been shed for our sins. Just as the children of Israel were not delivered from the destruction through their moral conduct but though their faith in the blood of the Passover, so too all who put their faith in Jesus receive complete forgiveness and reconciliation. "*In Christ God was reconciling the world to himself,*

20

not counting their trespasses against them .. and he made him to be sin who knew no sin, so that in him we might become the righteousness of God. (2 Corinthians 5:19,21 RSV)

2000 years ago, exactly on the day of Passover, Jesus fulfilled this feast by shedding His blood for all of us. His blood provides remission for the sins of the whole world. It remains for us to personally appropriate the benefits of His Passover by putting our faith in it. When we do this we enter into our personal Passover and receive forgiveness and reconciliation with God.

Passover prefigured the reality of Jesus' death. God passes over the sins of all who sincerely want to be reconciled with Him, forgiven and delivered from their sin. He allowed the innocent Lamb to bear the destruction our sins deserved.

As Isaiah foretold *"All we like sheep have gone astray we have turned everyone to his own way but the Lord has laid on him the iniquity of us all."* (Isaiah 53:6)

21

The most evil person can receive a new beginning in Jesus if he takes Jesus as His personal savior and applies the blood of Jesus to his life. *"God was in Christ, reconciling the world unto himself, not imputing their trespasses unto them; and hath committed unto us the word of reconciliation."* (2 Cor 5:19)

Since Jesus has historically and objectively fulfilled the Feast of Passover, we can say God has only two kinds of people on the earth: those sins are paid for and those who know it!! Our part is to repent and believe the good news and through His blood to be reconciled to God. When we personally recognize our need of the covering of the blood of Jesus for the remission of our sins and put our faith in it, we are forgiven and reconciled to God. This is our personal Passover from death to life.

How wonderful to come to Passover! If the first feast can bring us so much benefit what will be our state when we enter into the reality foreshadowed by each of the Feasts.

CHAPTER 3

FEAST OF UNLEAVENED BREAD

The feast of Unleavened Bread recalls the fact that the Children of Israel escaped captivity in Egypt and received a new destiny from God.

Not only did they survive the destruction that covered Egypt on the night of the Passover they were also emancipated from the rule of Egypt and liberated to embrace their new destiny.

They were in such a hurry to leave Egypt and begin their journey towards the Promised Land that there was no time for the leaven to be mixed with the dough. "*And they baked unleavened cakes of the dough which they had brought out of Egypt; for it*

23

was not leavened, because they were driven out of Egypt, and could not wait." (Exodus 12:39)

When we put our faith in Jesus we too are given a new destiny We are dead to our old destiny and, leaving behind our old lives, we can begin to live for God's purposes for our lives.

Many believers apply the blood of Jesus to their lives for the remission of sin and then go back to their old way of living. The children of Israel departed from Egypt immediately to move towards their new destiny.

As soon as we are born again through faith in Jesus we have a new destiny. We are removed from the dominion of Sin and the Devil in the same way as the children of Israel were removed from the dominion of slavery and of Pharaoh. We can now begin a new life liberated from the curses of our past under the dominion of Jesus.

"Therefore if any man is in Christ he is a new creation all things are passed away." Unleavened bread is a reminder that the redemption of Jesus is

more than forgiveness it is a transference into a whole new realm of living where we are given a new destiny and a new purpose. He has delivered us from the dominion of darkness and transferred us the dominion of His son. All who take Jesus as Savior must take him as Lord. We are now given over to the destiny, which our creator has always made us for.

Each person has two destines: His fallen destiny and God's new destiny for Him

We are all born under the dominion of darkness and unable to attain our real destiny in God. We all have disadvantages and blockages inherited from our genetics, our society, our condition and from our own fallen natures. All of these forces hold us from God's wonderful plan and destiny for us.

The Passover of Jesus breaks the power of our past to control us and opens up the door to God's plan and purpose for our lives. This is why Jesus is called "The Door". He is the blood-spattered door that shields us from destruction as the blood-spattered door shielded the children of Egypt on the night in Egypt long ago. He is also the door to our new destiny.

Unleavened Bread reminds us that believers have a door to a new destiny when we find new Life in the Messiah. We can break with our fallen misfortunate destiny and embrace the new destiny which the Lord sets before us. Jesus said: *"I set before you an open door that no man shut."* (Revelation 3:8)

To embrace Unleavened Bread is to embrace these realities and to break with fallen habits lifestyles and conditioning from our past life and to move towards the new destiny that God has for us.

Some believers try to hold on to their own lives, but that cuts them off from making further progress in God. The scriptures say that those who did not keep unleavened bread would be "cut off". This speaks of those who would hold on to their old lives and ways. Such people are cut off from making further progress in the kingdom of God.

26

Leaven is a symbol of sin. The leaven of sin came into all of us through our ancestral inheritance all the way back to Grandfather Adam. Paul tells us that sin entered the world through one man (Adam) and through one man (Jesus) it is removed (Romans 5:12) Jesus died on the Day of Passover and on the Day of Unleavened Bread He lay dead in the tomb.

The Feast of Unleavened Bread speaks of God's remedy for sin. Paul says that when Christ died we died (Romans 6:6). His plan is not only to *forgive* us of our sins but to *remove us from sin and sin from* us. Many people try to remove from their lives through religious means or through psychological techniques, but only Jesus can really remove us from its power.

> *Our Adam nature cannot be reformed but it can be replaced.*
>
> *Religion tries to improve the old but redemption replaces the old.*

Our Adam nature cannot be improved but it can be *replaced*. When we see that we died with Jesus we can lay our 'old man' down in His tomb and we can receive His life as the

27

replacement of our old Adam life. (Read carefully Romans Chapter 6, which speaks of the spiritual fulfillment of Unleavened Bread.)

Three elements are involved in our release from sin and the power of our old life.

- Knowing our old man was crucified with Christ, (Romans 6:6)

- Reckoning this to be a fact, (Romans 6:11) and

- Yielding ourselves to righteousness & refusing to yield to sin (Romans 6:12-14)

When a believer puts his faith on Jesus' death as the death of the sin nature, he fulfills the feast of Unleavened Bread because in Jesus' death he can put to death his old sin nature.

Unleavened Bread & Water Baptism

Our faith in Jesus as our Unleavened Bread i.e. in Jesus as the one who removes the leaven of sin should be expressed, by Water Baptism. Water Baptism is the 'funeral service' of the 'old man' i.e.

that part of our humanity which was governed by the sin principle. We express our emancipation from the Adam nature and the power of sin through baptism. The concept of baptism is identical to the Jewish practice of Mikvah, using water as a means of separating ourselves from impurity. The water of the Red Sea separated the children of Israel from their old life in Israel. The journey through the Red Sea was a sort of national mass Baptism. John preached Baptism for repentance and Christians use baptism (Mikvah) as a means of showing separation from the sin and uncleanness and curses associated with our past life.

On the Day of Unleavened Bread the children of Israel crossed the Red Sea leaving behind their old futile life and their bondage to Pharaoh. They did not return to work on the Pyramids the next day and share testimonies about the night before. They were on their way to a new life, and finished with their past life.

When we come to Christ we receive not only forgiveness for the sins of the past (Passover) but we come away from the domination of sin, our old lives, and demonic control. We are now free to live for the purposes for which God created us under the Lordship of Jesus.

Through our identification in Jesus sin has lost its power and dominion over us. We are still capable of sin of course as it still seeks to operate though our flesh and unsanctified habit patterns. However we now have power to resist it and not to become entangled in it because "*greater is He that is us than He that is in the world*"(I John 4:4)

Have you abandoned your old life to live for the purposes of God? Have you come to Unleavened Bread?

The Leavens Of The New Testament

Jesus (referring indirectly to the Feast of Unleavened Bread) warned His disciples to beware of "*the leaven of the Pharisees*", "*the leaven of the Saducees*" and the "*leaven of Herod*". (Matt. 16:6 &

Mark 8:15) These solemn words of Jesus are warnings to His followers of all generations. Leaven is a symbol of sin, and also of sinful influences. He warns of leavens or wrong teaching and practical influences, which would hinder us entering the Kingdom of God. Of the millions who put their faith on the blood of Jesus not all come to unleavened Bread and put off the leaven of the Adam life and these other leavens that Jesus speaks about.

The Leaven Of The Pharisees.

Jesus had many critical things to say against the Pharisees, but the spirit of the Pharisees has remained with believers throughout history and is a temptation to all of us. The Pharisees focused on external obedience rather than on inner righteousness. (Mark 7:3-4; Matt. 23:23)

Jesus is not against external observance but warns that *it is no substitute for inner righteousness.* He came to make us righteous *on the inside* by giving us His Spirit. Many today practice the externals of religious behavior but have no inner life and do little to ask the Lord to continue to change their hearts. They are participating in what Jesus calls: *"the leaven of the Pharisees'.* (Mark 8:15)

> *Beware of using external observance as a substitute for inner righteousness*

The Pharisees were noted for observing religious traditions meticulously. Jesus accused them of making void the word of God by their tradition. *'For laying aside the commandment of God you hold the tradition of men...making the word of God of no effect through your tradition'.* (Mark 7: 8 & 13) Traditions are not wrong but

- believers should not obey traditions that contradict the Word of God

- nor obey traditions as a substitute for obeying the Word of God.

Social cultural and religious traditions can enrich our lives but sometimes those traditions are in violation of the Word of God. Believers are exempt from observing all traditions that run against the spirit of the Word of God and should not consider themselves obligated to live by them. It is easy to conform to a religious culture Jewish, Catholic or Protestant etc. without any real living relationship with God, or any real inner transformation of our hearts. As Paul says *"neither circumcision nor uncircumcision avail but faith that works though love."*(Galatians 5:6)

One of the problems of adherence to tradition is that observance of traditions can deceive people into thinking that they are obeying God. Thus a Christian who goes to church on Christmas and Resurrection Day may think that he is a good Christian because he does these things. In fact there is nothing in the New Testament saying that we should observe Christmas and Resurrection Day, (though in our opinion it is a good thing to do). Observance of traditions and feasts are no indication of how closely we are following the Lord and yielding our lives to love Him and love others.

Traditions can easily become a smoke screen to deceive ourselves that we love God when in fact we are simply going through external motions that become a smoke screen to hide from ourselves the shallowness of our commitment to God and our need of repentance.

The Leaven of The Saducees

The Saducees were noted for their biblical exactness but were skeptical of the miraculous. They felt that the age of miracles was over and now with the scriptures to guide us that there was little need of the miraculous or the supernatural. Jesus chided them saying *'You know neither the scriptures nor the power of God.'* (Matt. 22:29)

They must have been quite insulted by this as they regarded themselves as the experts on the scriptures. They are not so different from believers today who study the Word of God and minimize the need of the miraculous intervention of God to sustain His people and to fulfil His word. A great section of the church has quenched the miraculous working of the Holy Spirit and justified this in the name of Bible Study.

Bible study should never be a substitute for belief in miracles, but should be a stimulus for faith. We study what God did in the past to know what we can expect of Him today. We are inspired to engage with the promise making, promise keeping God of power and might who has promised to never leave us or forsake us. How cold, flat, dull and boring Christianity becomes when the miraculous intervening power of God is minimized, feared and resisted.

The leaven of the Saducees has crept into Christianity where we have learnt to be excessively skeptical of the miraculous. *"Jesus Christ is the same yesterday today and forever."* (Hebrews 13:8) If we are to move on with God we are going to have to know the God of miracles. Our God works miracles to fulfill His promises for His followers. Today is the day of miracles! Throw out the leaven of the Saducees and live in expectation of great things from God!

Leaven Of Herod

There is no doubt that the leavens of the Pharisees and the Saducees have caused great damage to the progress of God's people, just as Jesus warned. But of all the leavens that He warned against, the leaven of Herod has probably done most to spoil the witness and life of the Church.

What is the "leaven of Herod"? Herod made cunning **political alliances** with the Roman Empire and sought through the political muscle of the Empire to further the cause of God. The result was an unholy alliance between political and spiritual power. When the church makes an unwholesome alliance with the political powers, relying on it to do its work for it, it is partaking of the Leaven of Herod. When it uses its influence to gain political power and loses its focus at making disciples it becomes weak and compromised. When the kingdom of God and the kingdom of the world

36

become merged in unholy compromise there is the leaven of Herod. Jesus kingdom is not of this world, and His ways will not take over the world until His return. The Leaven of Herod has often caused the witness of the church to be neglected for the sake of political influence.

At its beginning the church, like the people of Israel, were not a part of the nations. They marched to a different beat than the political alliances of the nations. They sought to worship and obey the living God. They were persecuted and ill treated because they were so different and their presence seemed to challenge the lifestyle of the world order in which they lived.

As the church spread throughout the Roman Empire and the countries of Europe it became embroiled in the political and social agenda of the nations it was a part of it. Believers began to adopt the social, cultural and political agenda of their nations rather than the agenda of the word of God. (For example the Christians in England, France

Spain and Germany fought for the agendas of their kings and so against one another. Their energies were spent not in serving the Lord and spreading His message but were sapped by serving the social cultural and political goals of their nations.) Christians fought Christians, when their nations fought each other and tyrannized tribal peoples when their nations tyrannized tribal people.

Worst of all, when the European nations adopted anti-Semitic postures, the Christians of those nations (being under the influence of the Leaven of Herod) followed the agenda of their political leaders and participated in the persecution of the Jewish people.

The New Testament teaches that believers should be loyal and good citizens in whatever nation they are a part of and should pray for their leaders. However their ultimate loyalty is to their the Lord and Savior, His Word and ways. We should be cautious of excessive patriotism lest we get carried off in a national agenda that are hostile to the ways and plan of God.

Jesus said *'Render therefore to Caesar the things that are Caesar's and to God the things that are God's.'* (Matt. 22:21) He recognized two entirely different spheres in which we live. Our duty to Caesar should never preempt our duty to God. Tragically a great percentage of believers render greater loyalty and expenditure of energy to Caesar than to God.

The Leaven Of Corinth

On two occasions in his letters, Paul exhorts his readers to get rid of leaven. Like Jesus, he uses the word 'leaven' as a metaphor for sinful influences that can spread like leaven among believers and corrupt our witness.

He warned the Corinthians to get rid of the leaven of sexual immorality from their church (1 Cor. 5:6) and he warned the Galatians to get rid of the leaven of legalism (Gal 5:9). Obviously sexual and other forms of immorality must be removed through the grace of God from our lives. Today's culture is not unlike that culture of Corinth.

We live in an age of extreme sexual permissiveness. Sexual immorality has become normal in our 21st century culture. Many who come to the Lord today (as in Paul's day) are coming into the Kingdom of God from a background of sexual permissiveness. We have learnt that God accepts us not on the ground of our conduct but on the ground of His Atoning sacrifice. In the light of this amazing grace some are tempted to believe that sexual immorality is now permissible. Paul says that we must get rid of all sexual immoral habits as this will destroy us.

Sexually transmitted disease threatens the lives not only of millions of unbelievers throughout the world but of millions of unbelievers. The teaching of grace should empower us to put sexual immorality (and all other immorality out of our lives). God does not want to be a spoil our fun - He wants to keep us alive in the face of habits of the world that threaten to destroy us. God gave sex to be enjoyed in His order as He designed us male and female.

For our own survival and because God requires it believers must learn to bring their sexual conduct under the control of the Holy Spirit. The leaven of Corinth (sexual immorality) is one of the greatest sources of misery among believers. Pastors, and those who disciple new believers, must handle their flocks with mercy but must help them to put away sexual immorality,

Failure to do so repels God's blessings and cuts off our spiritual life.

The Leaven Of The Galatians

Another leaven (influence) that Paul warned against was the leaven of relying on religious practices as means of sanctification. His warning is given in his Letter to the Galatians and so we call it the Leaven of the Galatians. *"O foolish Galatians! Who has bewitched you, before whose eyes Jesus*

41

Christ was publicly portrayed as crucified? Let me ask you only this: Did you receive the Spirit by works of the law, or by hearing with faith? Are you so foolish? Having begun with the Spirit, are you now ending with the flesh? Did you experience so many things in vain? --if it really is in vain. Does he who supplies the Spirit to you and works miracles among you do so by works of the law, or by hearing with faith? ..... So then, those who are men of faith are blessed with Abraham who had faith. For all who rely on works of the law are under a curse; for it is written, "Cursed be every one who does not abide by all things written in the book of the law, and do them."

If we rely on religious practices rather than on the facts of redemption and the working of the Holy Spirit to sanctify and produce godly character in us, we actually cut off the grace of God from our lives.

This temptation was an especially strong for Messianic Jews in Paul's day. They knew that they were justified through faith in Jesus' atoning sacrifice but were relying on religious observance for their sanctification. Today, unfortunately believers from religious Jewish and Christian backgrounds still tend to rely on the religious observance and cultural practices rather than on faith in God and His word to sanctify them.

Conclusion

The Feast of Unleavened Bread reminds us that God wants to remove sin from His people before He can move them on. God's people of the end days must avoid and reject all these leavens if it is to attain its high calling.

The scriptures say that those who did not remove leaven would be "cut off". (Exodus 12:19). Therefore if spiritual leavens are not removed the curses of separation from God will return. The anointings and blessings of God's presence will be removed from individuals and churches who do not remove the leavens from lives. Unless they are removed they will cut us off from further entry into the kingdom

The path of following the Lord and His Word is a path of life and not of death. It is an alternative lifestyle and way of living to that of the fallen world around us. Jesus' followers choose to live by this new lifestyle and love and choose to put off the agendas, methods and habits of the old life. The Feast of Unleavened Bread if observed in its reality would cause a revolution in the form, style, content and focus of the church.

Some may boast "We don't have this leaven or that one in our lives." However if we have *any* of the leavens in our midst the effect is the same. The leaven - all of it - must be removed.

In these days the Holy Spirit is removing the Leaven of the Pharisees, the leaven of the Saducees and the leaven of Herod from the church, the leaven of Corinth and the leaven of the Galatians from the church. Be sure that these leavens are taken from our lives.

The Feast Of First Fruits

The Feast of First Fruits commemorates the crossing of the Red Sea and the beginning of the life free of the dominion of Pharaoh and Egypt.

It is historically and objectively fulfilled in the ministry of Jesus when He rose on the day of the resurrection the first fruits of a new humanity emancipated from the slavery of sin and the dominion of darkness and the Prince of darkness.

Jesus rose on the Feast of First Fruits, again exactly fulfilling the exact pattern of the Feasts. He became the first fruits of the resurrection. *"But in fact Christ has been raised from the dead, the first fruits of those who have fallen asleep."* (1 Co 15:20)

On the day of His resurrection He breathed on the disciples and said to them: *"Receive the Holy Spirit"* (John 20:22) At that moment they received His Spirit into them. They received His resurrection life and were "born again" becoming New Creations.

45

When anyone puts his faith in the Resurrection of Jesus he can receive new life from Him. He enters into the first fruits of the New Life of the Kingdom of God. The life of the Spirit within the believer becomes a fountain of goodness and love flowing from His inmost being.

We begin our new life when we lay down our old life and receive the life of Jesus to be the controlling and liberating force of our lives. We are "born again" and begin a life emancipated from the control of the Devil, the agenda of sin and of the world, under the leadership of Jesus Our Good Shepherd. (We still can return to sin but we do not have to and will not as long as we abide in Jesus)

> *We are called not only to be forgiven sinners but transformed human beings*

The great gift of Jesus is not just remission of sin but the impartation of His life to us to be our life. He *"takes out the heart of stone and puts in a heart of flesh"* (Ezek. 36:26). He is reproducing a generation not only of forgiven sinners but of transformed human beings who have His sinless life flowing through them. His great gift to us is the Holy Spirit to live within us.

"If any one is in Christ he is a new creation the old is past away behold, the new has come." (2 Cor 5:17) When we put our faith in Jesus we come into union with Him in His death and resurrection. We are taken out of our slavery in Adam and brought into emancipation in Christ. Jesus is not only our Savior but also our Lord and Good Shepherd leading us on to our new blessed destiny.

CHAPTER 4

THE FEAST OF PENTECOST

The Feast of Pentecost was celebrated by The Jewish people in early summer as a celebration of the wheat harvest. This Feast also celebrates the giving of the law to Moses and the children of Israel at Mount Sinai to be their guide. The name Pentecost, (as we saw in the introduction) comes from the Greek word pentekoste (which means fiftieth). The Feast was called Pentecost in Greek because it came fifty days after Passover. The Jewish people call it Shavuot or the Feast of Weeks because it comes seven weeks after Passover.

Pentecost commemorates the great events of Sinai, which are recorded in Exodus. At that time

49

when Moses went up Mount Sinai to meet with the Lord,

- the mountain shook and was covered with darkness. (Exodus 19:16)

- fire came down on the mountain (Exodus 19:18)

- the law was written on tablets of stone. (Exodus 31:18)

When Moses came down the mountain he found the people worshipping a golden calf. In his anger he commanded the Levites to kill those who had participated in the idolatry and 3,000 were put to death that day. (Ex 32:28)

About fifteen hundred years later, Jesus fulfilled the Feast of Pentecost. He had promised His disciples that on the day of Pentecost they would be embued with 'power from on high' and baptized in the Holy Spirit.' (Acts 1:5; 2:1-4)

On the Day of Pentecost (Shavuot) after Jesus' Ascension, the city was crowded with pilgrims from many nations gathered in Jerusalem to celebrate the Feast. The disciples had gathered on Mount Zion to wait for the promised Holy Spirit. The place shook, fire came down and the law of love[1] was written on their hearts and not on tablets of stone. When Peter and the disciples came down and addressed the people 3,000 people, were made spiritually alive that day. (Acts 1 & 2)

It is extraordinary how many of the events of the first Pentecost on Mount Sinai were repeated in a different form on Mount Zion.

- At the first Pentecost Mount Sinai shook - at this Pentecost Mount Zion shook.

- At the first Pentecost fire came to write the Law on stone - at this Pentecost fire came to write (implant) the love of God into hearts - the law of the spirit of life.

- At the first Pentecost, on Mount Sinai, 3000 people were struck dead - at this Pentecost,

---

[1] Paul says that when we are justified by faith we have peace with God and His love is poured into our hearts by the Holy Spirit. (Romans 5:1-4) The pouring in of the love of God into our hearts by the Holy Spirit empowers us to live by the law of love, which is the fulfillment of the commandments. (1 Tim 1:5)

51

on Mount Zion, three thousand were made alive.

(We can rejoice that God has not given us a ministry of condemnation that leads to death but the ministry of the Spirit that leads to life!)

- At Sinai the children of Israel received the Law to be their guide, and now at Zion the Spirit is given to be our guide.

- Fifty days after the Passover, the children of Israel came to Sinai to receive the Law. Fifty days after Jesus' Resurrection the disciples received the empowerment of the Holy Spirit in Jerusalem on Mount Zion.

Because of the weakness of man's flesh they were unable to keep the righteous law that was given at Sinai. The Passover sacrifice of Jesus brought in eternal forgiveness and atonement for those who believe, repent, and acknowledge their need. Through the New Birth the Spirit of righteousness is placed within our hearts in fulfillment of the prophets.

Pentecost was fulfilled by Jesus when, on Mount Zion, He poured out His Spirit on His disciples (men and women) at the Feast of Pentecost. They received power to boldly proclaim Him and from then on their ministry was accompanied by the signs and mighty evidences of the working of the Holy Spirit.

> *All who come to Pentecost can present themselves to be clothed with the power of the Holy Spirit to live a life controlled by the Spirit of Jesus*

Jesus not only fulfilled Pentecost when He poured out His Spirit on the first 120 disciples. Each one of us can have a personal Pentecost. We can receive a personal Pentecost when we receive, by faith, from Jesus the Baptism in the Holy Spirit.

The disciples of Jesus had received forgiveness. They had put off their old lifestyle and had received Christ as their New Birth. Now they were looking for the anointing power to begin to reproduce the works of Jesus. Jesus had said to them "*He who believes in Me the works that I do, he shall do and greater works than these shall he do because I go to the Father.*" (John 14:34) When Jesus received the Holy Spirit to anoint Him for his ministry the heavens were opened to Him (Matt. 3:16).

Similarly, Pentecost opens the heavens in the life of a believer and he receives not only gifts but also the power through the Holy Spirit to do the works of God. It is not that we become powerful. It is that God's power accompanies us in our weakness.

When we give the Holy Spirit control of our lives, He leads us in the footsteps of Jesus and into all truth. All who come to Pentecost should commit to living by the teachings of Jesus and to be led by His Spirit of love. The Baptism in the Holy Spirit empowers us to love and serve as Jesus did, and opens the way for the miraculous working of the Holy Spirit to accompany our witness

The Baptism with the Holy Spirit is not an end but only the beginning of a life of obedience

54

and on-going change and discovery in the Kingdom of God. "*I have yet many things to say to you, but you cannot bear them now,*" says Jesus. '*When the Spirit of truth comes, He will guide you into all the truth: for He will not speak on His own authority, but whatever hears He will speak, and He will declare to you things that are to come. He will glorify Me, for he will take what is Mine and declare it to you.*" (John 16.12-14) The coming of the Holy Spirit would be the beginning of many discoveries for His disciples

On the Day of the Resurrection Jesus breathed His Spirit INTO His disciples. They were filled with the Spirit. On the day of Pentecost they were Baptized with the Holy Spirit. The Spirit now came UPON them. Jesus invites us all to come to Pentecost. He wants to anoint all, who have drunk of His Spirit, with the power to be His witnesses.

All who present themselves to live for God and to be His witnesses can by faith lay hold of this great gift of the Holy Spirit. We can receive His power to equip us to be his witness. Often we seek simply the equipment of education to do the works of God but this is limited, not sufficient and short of the provision that Jesus left to His followers... *"And it shall come to pass afterward, that I will pour out my spirit upon all flesh; and your sons and your daughters shall prophesy, your old men shall dream dreams, your young men shall see visions: And also upon the servants and upon the handmaids in those days will I pour out my spirit."* (Joel 2: 28-29)

"But ye shall receive power, after that the Holy Ghost is come upon you: and ye shall be witnesses unto me both in Jerusalem, and in all Judea, and in Samaria, and unto the uttermost part of the earth." (Acts 1:8)

This power must be appropriated by faith and by will. It is God' will for us to receive this power. It should be our will to lay hold of it and receive it by faith.

Today the Holy Spirit is restoring the reality of the Feast of Pentecost among believers and it is creating a revolution of power, witness and effectiveness throughout the world.

The Feast of Pentecost is a challenge to believers to build on our experience of salvation and new birth and receive the anointing and power to be instruments of God's grace and word to others.

During the Feast of Pentecost in Temple days the priests waved two loaves before the Lord. The two loaves are a wonderful picture of believing Jews and gentiles becoming one before God through the Messiah. The book of Ruth is read during Pentecost. It is a picture of the gentile being brought into the household of faith and blessing though marriage to Boaz the ancestor of David and Jesus. Pentecost opens up the way for the gospel to go to both Jew and Gentile and for the Gentile also to become partakers of the Blessing, through remission of sin, repentance and faith.

On the day of Pentecost the followers of Jesus received the first harvest of the Kingdom of God and 3000 people were added to the congregation. Within a few years the good news of the kingdom had spread throughout the known world through the Jews of the Diaspora and to

Gentiles who also were reconciled to God. This first harvest is the precursor of the great ingathering harvest, which will occur at the end of the age.

CHAPTER 5

THE FEAST OF TRUMPETS

At the Feast of Trumpets, trumpets are sounded summoning people to get ready for the days that are ahead. The feast recalls and commemorates the entry of the children of Israel under the headship of Joshua into the Promised Land. (Joshua Chapter 6) This feast is known in Hebrew as Yom Turah, the Day of Trumpets or the Day of Alarm. It is also know as Rosh Hashanah, the head of the year, as it marks the beginning of the new civil year for Israel.

In ancient Israel trumpets were blown to

- alert people to an impending danger,

- to summon people to assemble together in unity for warfare,

- and to prepare to advance.

The Feast of Trumpets is a preparation for Tabernacles. It comes at the first day of the seventh month the climax of the Lord's Year. Trumpets then is a preparation feast for the other two all feasts Atonement and Tabernacles

It summons people to get ready for the awesome and glorious days of this seventh month— Tabernacles (Sukkoth) the climax of the Jewish year anticipating the climax of history and redemption.

Since the Feast of Tabernacles (as we shall see) will be historically and objectively fulfilled by Jesus on His return to earth, the Feast of Trumpets anticipates events that will awaken us to the fact that the Day of the Lord's return is coming.

Certain events will take place in Israel and in the world that will alert believers to the fact that the return of the Lord is near. These events are the

60

historical fulfillment of the feast of Trumpets, as they are a wake up call to the earth and especially to believers to prepare for the (second) coming of the Lord.

Jesus said that we could discern certain signs in the events of history, which would enable us to know that His Return was near. He told us that (though we would not know the exact day or hour of His return) we would be able to discern the *season* of His return. Various discernible signs would precede His coming.

His followers asked Him what would be the signs of His coming and of the end of the age. (Matthew 24:1-3) The "end of the age" is the end of the age which was inaugurated by Jesus coming and which will conclude on His return.

Jesus prophesied four things concerning Jerusalem and the Jewish People. When these four things are fulfilled we would know that His coming is very near.

The Four signs concerning Jerusalem that would precede His coming are

(1) the destruction of the city (Luke 21:20)
(2) the destruction of the Temple (Matt. 24:2)
(3) the scattering of the people among the nations
(4) the return of the City to Israeli control. (Lk.: 21:24)

Jesus said: "*Jerusalem will be trodden down underfoot by the Gentiles until he times of the Gentiles are fulfilled.*" The phrase '*until the times of the Gentiles are fulfilled*' (Luke 21:24) means "until Gentile domination of

> **The return of Jerusalem to the Jewish people is a trumpet summoning us to prepare for the return of the Lord**

the City of Jerusalem comes to and end". Jesus said that when the City returned to Jewish control we should *"Look up and lift your heads, because your redemption draws near."* (Lk 21:28)

In 1967 the City of Jerusalem (for the first time since its destruction in 70 AD) came back under Israeli control. This fulfills the prophetic word of

Jesus in Luke 21:24. The regathering of Israel to their land and the restoration of Jerusalem to Jewish control are the great historic events, which signal His soon coming. They are loud signals to the nations that tell us the Lord's coming is close.

Surely these events are the preparation events that signal His return and by which we can know His coming is near. We must therefore consider that the regathering of Israel and the return of Jerusalem to their control is the objective fulfillment of the Feast of Trumpets. Jesus said that when the Jews return to Israel we would know we are at the end of the age.

In the parables of the wheat and the tares (Luke chapter 13) Jesus said that the end of the age is the time of the Harvest. In other words the retun of the Jewish people to Jerusalem will be a signal that we are at the time of the final harvest of History.

The Feast of Trumpets however is more than an alarm that lets us know God's season. It is also a call to prepare.

The generation on the earth since 1967 is the first generation EVER that can intelligently hope for the Return of the Lord in their lifetime, since it is the first generation that has seen Jerusalem back in Israeli control. This means that God is calling this generation to:

(1) to be ready (i.e. to hear the trumpet) for His appearing;
(2) to stand with God's purposes for Israel and the nations;
(3) to make the spiritual preparations that are necessary

The historic events of our day make us realize that we are approaching God's great harvest season and the climax of history. .

In the parable of the wise and foolish virgins Jesus spoke about two sections of His followers. One part would ignore the signs of is coming and miss the opportunity and time.

The awareness that we are in the time of the end should not summon us to speculation but to dedicate ourselves more intensely to work in the harvest and purifying ourselves for the Lord's return. It is time for the wise virgins' to have their lamps burning brightly and hear the wake up call' announcing the coming of the Bridegroom. (See Mt. 25)

The Feast of Trumpets in the life of the Christian is fulfilled when he spiritually hears the call to move on in the Spirit, to prepare for spiritual battles, and to take his place in the harvest work.

At the First Trumpets when Joshua and the children of Israel conquered the land, the Lord appeared to Joshua as the Commander of the Lord's army. Joshua asked Him, '"*Are You for us or for our adversaries?" So He said, " No but as Commander of the army of the Lord I have now come.*"' (Joshua 5:13-14) At Trumpets we learn to cease from trying to co-opt God for our agenda but instead we bring our lives into conformity to His will. Trumpets commemorates Jewish return to their homeland. As we enter to the reality behind this feast we align ourselves with God's purpose for

Israel and the nations that is being worked out through the return of Israel to their land in God's plan.

The believer enters his personal subjective trumpets when he recognizes the reality of the coming of the Lord and gives himself for the agenda of the Lord in these end days. His great agendas in these days are

- the restoration of the Jewish people to their land,

- the end time harvest of the nations and the sanctification and preparation of His followers.

The trumpets of the Old Testament summoned people to prepare for things to come and to prepare for war. We fulfill the Feast of Trumpets when we allow the Holy Spirit to rouse us to be alert, aware of the signs of the times and ready for the return of the Lord, and to be actively hastening the day of His coming. We also fulfill this feast when we do not rest on the laurels of the new birth and the Baptism with the Holy Spirit but press on through greater and greater surrender, to perfection.

Trumpets is the place of counting the cost, waking up from our religious complacency *"Therefore gird up your minds, be sober, set your hopefully upon the grace that is coming to you at the revelation of Jesus the Messiah."* (1 Peter 1: 13) Peter here is sounding the trumpet note to his readers.

Paul, too, shows that he has heard that trumpet calling him upward and onward when he writes: *"Not that I have already obtained this or am already perfect; ... but one thing I do, forgetting what lies behind and straining forward to what lies ahead. I press on toward the goal for the prize of the upward call to God in Christ Jesus."* (Ph 3:12-15)

'Therefore let us leave the elementary doctrine of Christ and go on to maturity, not laying again a foundation of repentance from dead works and of faith toward God, with instruction about

ablutions, the laying on of hands, the resurrection from the dead, and eternal judgment." (Heb. 6:1-2)

Here again the trumpet note is being sounded to the church to move on from elementary things towards the perfection to which we are called. We do not to leave these foundations behind in the sense that we do not need them any more, but we are to build on the foundation of what we have already entered into.

> The Feast of Trumpets summons us to aggressive faith and overcoming obedience

Awakening For Spiritual Warfare

The Feast of Trumpets marks the transition of the Children of Israel from the era of being sustained by God's provision in the wilderness, to a time when they would have to be more aggressive in their lives as they moved into the Promised Land and overcame their enemies. The Christian life is a life of rest based on the finished work of Jesus. However, as we respond to the call and purposes of God for our lives, we cannot be passive but must seek to obey and not be deterred from God's plan by fears or obstacles

Believers abide by faith in God's provision but at the same time we must learn to resist the spirits, which would try to keep us from our inheritance. As Jesus resisted the voice of the devil during His period in the wilderness, so believers must learn to silence the voice of evil spirits that bring discouragement, unforgiveness, bitterness and that seek to "steal, kill and destroy" our peace, purpose and provision." (John 10:10)

"The thief comes to steal kill and destroy says Jesus but I am come that you may have life and have it more abundantly." (John 10:10)

At the Feast of Trumpets the children of Israel began to enter the Promised Land and to overcome every force that kept them from their inheritance.

In the same way we can learn to expel attitudes and spirits that keep us from the love, joy, peace, provision and direction of the Kingdom.

69

"Resist the devil and he will flee." (James 4:7) God is summoning His people to move beyond passive trust to active overcoming faith. Jesus has given His followers the authority to expel demons that resist us on earth as we go forward to do his will. (Mark 16:16) *"Behold I give you authority over all the works so the enemy and nothing shall in any way harm You."*

Believers must do more than passively trust the Lord for His blessings. We must resist attitudes and spirits that seek to steal from us emotionally spiritually, physically and mentally. We do this by renouncing wrong attitudes and by commanding oppressing spirits to cease from their activity against us.

As we learn the lesson of Trumpets we learn that spiritual warfare is a part of every believers walk. (We should not become devil conscious but conscious of God's inheritance and be able to resist thoughts and spirits that are hostile to His benign purposes for us.)

Trumpets & Israel

At Trumpets we awake to and align ourselves with God's purposes for Israel. We recognize that just as Israel has been separated from its land, the church has been separated from its roots in Israel. We recognize the tragic effects of anti-Semitism in Church history. We can repent of this tragic sin and become active participants in what God is doing on the earth, by blessing Israel in practical ways.

Throughout history the church has become enmeshed in the political agendas of the nations in which it was scattered which resulted in our participation in the anti-Semitism of the nations. As God calls Israel again out of the nations back to its Promised Land, the church is challenged to align itself with God's historic agenda rather than the agenda of the nations.

"He will set up a banner for the nations, and will assemble the outcasts of Israel and gathered

together the dispersed of Judah from the four corners of the earth." (Isaiah 11:12)

Ezekiel prophesied that the end time regathering of Israel would result in their spiritual resurrection. *"Then you shall know that I am the Lord when I have opened your graves, O My people and brought you up out of your graves. I will put my Spirit in you, and you shall live, I will place you in your own land. Then you shall know that I the Lord have spoken it and performed it says the Lord."* (Ezekiel 37:12-14)

Paul reminds us that though the Jewish people for the most part have not accepted the New Covenant, they are still God's chosen people on the basis of the Abrahamic Covenant.

"And if some branches were broken off, and you being wild branches were grafted in ..., and with them became partakers of the root and fatness of the olive tree, do not boast against the branches .. you do not support the root, but the root supports you concerning the gospel they are enemies for your sake, but concerning election they are beloved

72

for the sake of the fathers. For the gifts and calling of God are irrevocable." (Romans 11:17-19, 28-29)

CHAPTER 6

THE DAY OF ATONEMENT

The Day of Atonement - Yom Kippur, follows the Feast of Trumpets. It is not a feast day but a fast day - *"a day of repentance and affliction of soul."*

In the days of the Temple it was the most solemn day of the year. It was the only day of the year when the High Priest appeared in the Holy of Holies to offer sacrifice first for Himself and then for the sins of his people. Two goats were taken, and after lots were cast, one was chosen to be slain as a blood sacrifice, and the other, the scapegoat, was led outside the camp into the wilderness.

(Leviticus 16) The High Priest made atonement for the sins of the people of Israel by presenting the blood of the slain goat before the Lord in the Holy of Holies. He then would confess over the head of the scapegoat the sins of the nation and symbolically transfer the guilt of the people of Israel to the scapegoat.

This is similar to Passover which is also a day of transferring sin from people to a lamb. The emphasis on Passover is on *individual* repentance, while the emphasis on The Day of Atonement has an additional emphasis of *national* repentance, and cleansing.

The Day of Atonement repeats the themes of Passover and amplifies them. Man's guilt and God's provision of Atonement is the greatest theme of the Bible from Genesis to Revelation. In fact the Book of Revelation portrays Jesus as the Lamb slain for the sins of the world before the foundation of the world. Throughout all ages worship is given to Him

> **Man's guilt and God's provision of Atonement is the greatest theme of the Bible from Genesis to Revelation**

who has reconciled men from every tribe and tongue and people and nation to God. (Rev. 5:9) The atoning work of the Lamb is not only the central fact of History it is the central fact of eternity

The Feasts of Passover and Unleavened Bread symbolize the covering and the removal of sin. Atonement also contains these two themes

- the covering of sin represented by the blood of the animal sprinkled on the Mercy Seat in the Holy of Holies and

- The removal of sin and its consequences (including guilt, grief, sorrow and sickness) symbolized by the goat that is led into the wilderness.

A gospel that offers the covering of sin without its removal is not faithful to the Biblical themes of Atonement.

The leading out of the goat out into the wilderness on the Day of Atonement anticipated the great Day when the Lord took on Himself the sins and sicknesses of the world.

Not only are our sins forgiven, they are *taken away* from us. It is our responsibility

- to detest our sins,

- have the guilt of that sin covered and

- have the sins removed from our lives.

The Lord can only cover those sins that are renounced and laid on Him, and can only bear away sins that are placed on Him to be removed from our lives.

YOM KIPPUR & ISAIAH 53

Who has believed our report? and to whom is the arm of the LORD revealed?
For he shall grow up before him as a tender plant, and as a root out of a dry ground: he has no form nor comeliness; and when we shall see him, there is no beauty that we should desire him.
He is despised and rejected of men; a man of sorrows, and acquainted with grief: and we hid as it

were our faces from him; he was despised, and we esteemed him not.

Surely he hath borne our griefs (sicknesses), and carried our sorrows (pains): yet we esteemed him stricken, smitten of God, and afflicted.

But he was wounded for our transgressions, he was bruised for our iniquities: the chastisement of our peace was upon him; and with his stripes we are healed.

All we like sheep have gone astray; we have turned every one to his own way; and the LORD hath laid on him the iniquity of us all.

He was oppressed, and he was afflicted, yet he opened not his mouth: he is brought as a lamb to the slaughter, and as a sheep before her shearers is dumb, so he opened not his mouth.

He was taken from prison and from judgment: and who shall declare his generation? For he was cut off out of the land of the living: for the transgression of my people was he stricken.

And he made his grave with the wicked, and with the rich in his death; because he had done no violence, neither was any deceit in his mouth.

Yet it pleased the LORD to bruise him; he has put him to grief: when you shall make his soul an offering for sin, he shall see his seed, he shall prolong his days, and the pleasure of the LORD shall prosper in his hand.

He shall see of the travail of his soul, and shall be satisfied: by his knowledge shall my righteous servant justify many; for he shall bear their iniquities. (Isaiah 53:1-12)

This passage foretells how the Messiah would come and take on Himself the sins of Israel and of the world. The most important thing about Jesus is not that He was a great teacher or prophet but that He was the innocent Lamb of God who provided Atonement for Israel and the whole world. Jesus was sentenced to death in the precincts of the temple and led in the path of the scapegoat across the Kidron valley to be crucified on the Mount of Olives.

The two aspects of the day of Atonement the animal slain to cover the sins of the people and the scapegoat being led away to take away the sins and iniquities, guilts, sorrows, griefs and rejections of the people

As believers in the atoning sacrifice of Jesus we should release to Jesus our scapegoat all our griefs sorrow, guilts, rejections, sickness and pains. We should do this frequently in prayer and especially at Holy Communion when we remember the Lord's death for us. Many are bound by guilt, sorrow, pain, grief and sickness because they have not released these hurts to be borne away by Jesus as foreshadowed by the ritual of the day of Atonement and the prophecy of Isaiah 53.

Day of Atonement & National Repentance

On the Day of Atonement the High Priest made sacrifice for his own sins and the sins of the *nation*. Many Jewish people rely simply on the fact that they are children of Abraham and part of the chosen people for their salvation,

The Day of Atonement like the Day of Passover reminds us that Biblical Faith demands that all men renounce their sins and receive covering for them and put them away.

The Day of Atonement also anticipates the day when the people of Israel will put aside their sins and enter into National Repentance. The people of Israel (who are now without Temple sacrifice) will then place all their sins on the Lamb of God and eternal Scapegoat Atonement Jesus. Then the nation shall be saved. National revival and repentance will come on Israel, and the people of Israel will become a righteous nation. The curses arising from their disobedience will be removed and they will be fully reconciled with God the Father through the Atoning work of Messiah Jesus.

"Who has heard such a thing? Who has seen such things? Shall a land be born in one day? Shall a nation be brought forth in one moment? For as soon as Zion was in labor she brought forth her

sons." (Isaiah 66:8) Isaiah, and later the apostle Paul, foresaw the day when Israel.

- will return to the Lord,

- believe in the Atonement God has provided for the covering and removal of their sins and

- be cleansed of all their guilt and iniquity.

'And so all Israel will be saved; as it is written, "The Deliverer will come from Zion, he will banish ungodliness from Jacob"; "and this will be my covenant with them when I take away their sins." (Romans 11:26-27 & Isaiah 59:20-21)

Though permanent atonement was provided 2000 years ago, the national repentance of Israel has not yet happened.

Soon the Jewish people as a nation will turn and receive the benefits of this redemption. That is why the Day of Atonement comes after the day of trumpets because the national repentance of Israel will follow their regathering.

83

Ezekiel clearly shows the regathering of Israel will be followed by their national repentance and their recognition of their Messiah King. "*For I will take you from the nations, and gather you from all the countries, and bring you into your own land. I will sprinkle clean water upon you, and you shall be clean from all your uncleanness, and from all your idols I will cleanse you. A new heart I will give you and a new spirit I will put within you; and I will take out of your flesh the heart of stone and give you a heart of flesh. And I will put my spirit within you, and cause you to walk in my statutes and be careful to observe my ordinances. You shall dwell in the land, which I gave to your fathers; and you shall be my people, and I will be your God.*" (Ezekiel 36:24-28 RSV)

Atonement Foreshadows the Resurrection

Jesus perfectly fulfilled Atonement when He died on Calvary and His resurrection is the evidence that His sacrifice was acceptable. When the High Priest went into the Holy of Holies on the Day of

Atonement to offer sacrifice for the sins of the people the only way people had of knowing that the sacrifice was accepted was if he came out from the Holy of Holies to tell them. Without the Resurrection we would not know that Jesus' sacrifice for sin was accepted.

Jesus who brought His own blood into the sanctuary of Heaven exactly fulfilled this picture. His resurrection is the evidence that His sacrifice was accepted. When He appeared to His disciples on the day of His resurrection He showed them the nail prints in His hands. This was the evidence that the same Jesus who was crucified now stood alive before them. Then He said *"Peace be with You"* *"Shalom."* He could give them His peace because His eternal sacrifice was eternally accepted. (See John 21;19-21)

Since the resurrection is a *fact* of History and not simply a *belief* of Christians we know that the sins of the world have been atoned for. It remains for the nations and for Israel to put their faith in this reality and to release their guilt to the Lamb who has atoned for the sins of the world sins through repentance on faith.

The Day of Atonement shows that God calls not only *individuals* to repentance but *nations* to come to repentance. The thrust of global evangelism should be directed towards nations as well as to individuals.

Atonement & Purification

The scriptures tell us that Jesus is coming for a bride without spot or wrinkle (Ephesians 5:25-27) and so His coming is preceded by an intense purifying of the church. The Day of Atonement also typifies and anticipates the work of the Lord in purifying His Bride.

Peter was referring to believers at this stage of their Christian walk when he wrote: *'Beloved, do not be surprised at the fiery ordeal which comes upon you to prove you, as though something strange were happening to you. But rejoice and be glad when His glory is revealed. If you are reproached for the name of Christ, you are blessed, because the*

86

spirit of glory and of God rests upon you. But let none of you suffer as a murderer or a thief, or a wrongdoer or a mischief-maker; yet if one suffers as a Christian, let him not be ashamed, but under that name let him glorify God. For the time has come for judgment to begin with the household of God; and if it begins with us, what will be the end of those who do not obey the gospel of God?" (1 Peter 4:12-17)

Peter is urging believers to get ready for the Lord's return. The suffering that they are going through is not a judgment of condemnation, but a crisis for their purification. Crises and difficulties reveal vestiges of sin: pride, worldliness, vanity, greed, fear etc. that still cling to us. We can recognize these defects as sin and remove them from ourselves by laying them on the Lamb and renouncing them. This further application of atonement (refining) prepares us for the final harvest of our personal redemption and for the triumphant return of Yeshua.

87

There are certain forms of suffering from which the Christian is exempt, and which he does well to resist. There is however, another form of suffering, which is a suffering of purification. This can come in any form the Lord allows, and to resist in this case would be to resist God. This is an important area for discernment. We need to know how to resist the devil and all that he would throw against us, but we also need to know when to humble ourselves under the hand of God. *"Humble yourselves therefore under the mighty hand of God, that in due time he may exalt you."* (1 Peter 5:6)

This process in our spiritual advance corresponds to the Jewish feast of Atonement. It fulfills in reality what Yom Kippur foreshadows. This Atonement purification stage is only a transition stage in the process of being led to full maturity by the Holy Spirit. This stage is preparing us for a greater revelation of the glory of God. *"This slight momentary affliction prepares us for an eternal weight of glory beyond all comparison."* (2 Cor. 4:17) *"Jesus, for the joy that was set before him endured the cross, despising the shame."* (Hb. 12:2)

The suffering of refinement prepares us for a greater revelation of God's glory to us and in us. As God prepares us for the final stages of our redemption, the heat of the refiner's fire is felt with great intensity This is not the suffering of sin, defeat or unbelief, but the suffering of those who are being refined by the fire of the Holy Spirit. Jesus baptizes us with the Holy Spirit and with fire. This refining fire cleanses us of all impurities and fleshiness to get us ready for the return of the Lord, and for the final phase of our redemption.

John the Baptist said: *'I baptize you with water for repentance, but he who is coming after me is mightier than I whose sandals I am not worthy to carry; He will baptize you with the Holy Spirit and WITH FIRE. His winnowing fork is in his hand, and he will clear his threshing floor and gather his wheat into the granary, but the chaff he will burn with unquenchable fire."* (Matt. 3:12)

89

This fire burns the chaff of impurity out of the lives of those who are moving on in Christ, and getting ready for the 'glory that is to be revealed.' *"Furthermore, we have had human fathers who corrected us, and we paid them respect. Shall we not much more readily be in subjection to the Father of spirits and live? For they indeed for a few days chastened us as seemed best to them, but He for our profit that we may be **partakers of His holiness.**"* (Hebrews 12:9-10)

The refining work of the Day of Atonement prepares us for the glory and harvest of the Feast of Tabernacles. A church without the refiner's fire is a church without a harvest.

Atonement & Armageddon

The Day of Atonement also speaks graphically of the judgment of the nations, which will come immediately before the Lord's enthronement. When He returns He will judge the nations and separate them like a shepherd separating sheep and goats. (Matt 25:31-46) This alludes to the ceremony of the Day of Atonement and predicts an awesome judgment of the nations on His return.

The Day of Atonement anticipates the events spoken of in the book of Revelation as the Battle of Armageddon. (Rev. 16:16) *"But the day of the Lord will come as a thief in the night, in which the heavens will pass away with a great noise, and the elements will melt with fervent heat."* (2 Peter 3:10) (The word "elements" here translates the Greek word "stoicheion" which means "systems" .)

The scriptures do not predict the destruction of the planet but the destruction of the present systems, which rule the earth. The plan of God is not to destroy the world but to redeem it. The present economic, political and social world order or systems will be "destroyed" at the coming of the Lord and replaced by the perfect system of the Kingdom of

> *Atonement anticipates the destruction of the present systems which rule the earth today*

91

God, ruled over by Messiah. Man's "new world order" will be replaced by the Lord's world order.

Psalm 100 was sung on the Day of Atonement. It exhorts us to *"Enter His gates with thanksgiving, and His courts with praise: be thankful unto Him and bless His name."* (Psalm 100:4) How much more should we sing His praises in the light of the fulfillment of Atonement.

It is not the purpose of this book to speculate about unfulfilled Biblical Prophecy. The pattern of the Feasts together with the words of the prophets indicate that Israel's return (Trumpets) will be followed by a time of tribulation during which the nation shall come to the Lord and find national repentance and cleansing through faith in the Atoning Sacrifice Jesus .

May we also submit to His cleansing processes and so prepare to be *the "bride without spot or wrinkle"* ready to meet the Bridegroom at His triumphant return to fulfill the Feast of Tabernacles.

CHAPTER 7

THE FEAST OF TABERNACLES

The Feast of Tabernacles is the final and most joyful of the Jewish Feasts. It recalls the events in the history of Israel when the children of Israel dwelt in tents or booths - simple shelters made from the branches of trees. Though without any normal means of economic support God Himself provided for their every need.

During the Feast of Tabernacles the Jewish people erect booths made of leafy branches, on their rooftops, yards or balconies and eat there recalling the faithfulness God to provide in all circumstances and economies for His people.

The first Tabernacles took place in the wilderness but the original plan of God was for the children of Israel to be in their land by the time of harvest. It is a feast of celebration and rest, which celebrates God's faithfulness to fulfill His promises, bring the people to their land, and meet with them in fellowship peace and blessing.

The Feast of Tabernacles is also known as the Feast of Ingathering or Harvest. It looks back to the seminal events in Israel's history when God provided for them in the wilderness. However it also points to the conclusion and fulfillment of God's plan for them and for the nations - the climax of redemption.

Something Left Unfinished

"So when they had come together, they asked him, "Lord, will you at this time restore the kingdom to Israel?" He said to them, "It is not for you to know times or seasons which the Father has fixed by his own authority. But you shall receive

power when the Holy Spirit has come upon you; and you shall be my witnesses in Jerusalem and in all Judea and Samaria and to the end of the earth." (Acts 1:6-8)

The disciples knew that there was an aspect of Jesus' Messianic work that was not yet finished. Israel's kingdom had not yet been restored nor was Jesus reigning in triumph over the nations.

The redemption of the world and the completion of the believers' redemption are intertwined. Both events are linked to the return of the Lord and the establishment of His throne in Jerusalem.

Jesus has not yet historically and objectively fulfilled the Feast of Tabernacles because it anticipates the final events of the age:

1) the return of Messiah, His enthronement on the royal seat of David
2) the completion of the redemption and
3) the inauguration of the Messianic Age.

At that time, He who came first as a "Lamb" will return in triumph as the "Lion of Judah". *"The kingdoms of this world will become the kingdoms of our Lord and of His Messiah, and He shall reign forever and ever."* (Rev. 11:15)

This event will be preceded by the collapse and breakdown of the present world systems and will result in the outer establishment of the Lord's kingdom.

Though He told us we do not "*know the times or the seasons, which the Father hath put in his own power.*" (Acts 1:7) Jesus also told us that when we see the Jewish people back in control of the city of Jerusalem we should prepare for the hour of redemption. (Luke 21:24) This is the redemption of the earth and of the whole creation. Paul speaks about it in the eight chapter of Romans; *"the whole creation groans and labors with birth pangs together until now. Not only that but we also who have the first fruits of the spirit even we ourselves groan within ourselves eagerly waiting for the adoption, the redemption of our body."* (Romans 8:22-23)

The early Christians lived in constant expectation of the return of the Lord. *"To those who eagerly wait for Him, He will appear a second time apart from sin for salvation."* (Heb. 9:28) Their expectation was not only for the return of the Lord but for the completion of redemption.

The Feast OF Tabernacles - A Lesson in Hope

The pattern of the Feasts of the Lord enables us to see the future events of history in the context of the fulfillment of God's great plan for world redemption.

> *Tabernacles anticipates the Redemption of the whole creation at the Lord's return*

Unfortunately much of end time teaching among Christians has focused on the impending judgements and the tribulations that will mark the end of the age. While aware of the place of tribulation, our focus should

97

be on the glorious outcome. God will send Messiah Jesus back to this earth to

- complete our redemption,
- to bind the devil and
- transform this earth into a Paradise of peace under His loving firm and benign rule from Jerusalem.

Though we have experienced the fulfillment of Passover and Pentecost, we still await an even more glorious moment in history. We who now have the "first fruits of the Spirit" will then receive the fullness of our redemption (Romans 8:23). We shall welcome Jesus back to Jerusalem (Hb 9:28). His feet will stand on the Mount of Olives (Zech. 14:4). He will overthrow every rule and authority that has held the peoples of the world in bondage. (Rev. 11:15) He will come to claim the throne of David and bring in everlasting peace and righteousness to the nations.

At that time the believers who are alive on the earth will

- be glorified,

- receive the redemption of our bodies,

- rise to met him in the air and

- return to reign and rule with Him.

His overcomers will sit with Him on His throne and rule reign with Him. (I Cor 15:5152; I Thess. 4:17; Rev. 3:21) *"Therefore gird up your minds, be sober, set your hope fully upon the grace that is coming to you at the revelation of Jesus Christ."* (1 Peter 1:13) the message of the retun o f the Lord is not a message of doom and gloom but of great hope and redemption. Believers have the greatest message of hope to offer to the people of this world. Yes a warning of destruction for those who ignore God's help and resources but a promise of great joy for those who eagerly ·obey Him and look to Him.

During the Feast of Tabernacles Israel was commanded to "rejoice before the Lord for seven days" (Lev 23:4)) Tabernacles anticipates the greatest time of joy and redemption that is ahead for us at the coming of the Lord.

Tabernacles - Harvest Of Personal Redemption

This final stage of our redemption will bring us to full maturity in Christ. Today the nature of Christ in every born again believer is partly hidden by the veil of our own flesh. Paul speaks of *"Christ in us the hope of glory."* (Colossians 1:27) The presence of Christ in us is a promise of an even greater glory. The gift of the Holy Spirit is not the end but the down payment on an even greater glory that is to be revealed in us at the right time (Ephesians 1:14).

We have already received the Holy Spirit, but the best is yet to be for believers. As amazing as the New Birth is, as joyous as the Pentecost gift of the Holy Spirit is, there is yet a greater stage of our redemption ahead of us. *"It is in this hope that we have been saved."* (Rom. 8:24) The gift of forgiveness, New Birth and of the Baptism in the Holy Spirit can be received through faith. The full breaking out of God's glory in us, and the full redemption of our bodies[2] cannot be claimed by faith, but anticipated in hope.

"So Christ, having been offered once to bear the sins of many, will appear a second time, not to deal with sin but to save those who are eagerly waiting for him." (Heb. 9:28 RSV)

Paul writes: *"I consider that the sufferings of this present time are not worth comparing with the glory that is to be revealed in us. For the creation waits with eager longing for the revealing of the sons of God;... We know that the whole creation has been groaning in travail together until now; and not only the creation but we ourselves, who have the first fruits of the Spirit, groan inwardly as we wait*

---

[2] In scripture the word "tabernacle" or "tent" is used as a metaphor for the body.. The Feast of Tabernacles anticipates the redemption of our bodies.

101

for adoption as sons, the redemption of our bodies. For in this hope were we saved." (Romans 8:18-24)

All this is pre-figured by the Feast of Tabernacles. It is the feast of greatest joy in which the full harvest and the conclusion of the agricultural year is celebrated. It points to a time when God will reap the full harvest of redemption, and we will come to full ripeness and maturity as believers.

"Beloved, we are God's children now; it does not yet appear what we shall be, but we know that when he appears we shall be like him, for we shall see him as he is. And every one who thus hopes in him purifies himself as he is pure." (I John 3:2-3)

Tabernacles & God's Provision

As we have seen, throughout the Feast the Jewish people live in booths which they construct with branches of various trees and decorate with fruit. Dwelling in booths at the time of harvest is a reminder that no matter how much we may have prospered and how full our barns may be we remain

102

entirely dependent on God. The flimsy booths remind us of this dependence and of the Lord's provision. The more we are enriched by God the more humble we should be.

In today's world people are told to seek financial independence but Tabernacles reminds us that the greatest security, financially and every way is to be completely dependent on the Lord. We are never closer to the Lord than when we are most dependent on Him.

During the harvest festivals Israel was also commanded not to 'glean' the corners of the field and to leave something for the poor and for the stranger. (Leviticus 23:22) Always as we celebrate the goodness of the Lord we are to remember the poor. As God's love flows *to* us it should also overflow *from* us.

This is another reason that God reminds us at the feasts to remember the poor and the stranger. We are not the source of our own prosperity and blessings. It is God who has opened His hand over our lives. As we who were born in slavery have received blessing after blessing from Him we should also have open hands for the needy of the world.

God Reveals Himself In Time

The full harvest of our redemption will come at the return of Yeshua. He came and fulfilled The Feast of Passover in the 'fullness of time' at the time that was pre-ordained by the Father, not a day sooner or later. His death on the cross in the thirty-third year of His life on earth came exactly at Passover. The promise of the Feast of Pentecost was also fulfilled at precisely the right time: -'when the day of Pentecost was fully come' (Acts 2:1) So too He will come to fulfill the Feast of Tabernacles at the preordained time. As we have seen the disciples asked Jesus about this time but He did not tell them.

God inhabits eternity but moves with precise timing in history. Before the resurrection of Jesus no one could receive the new birth because, as John says, "as yet the spirit was not given". Before the Pentecost that followed Jesus' resurrection no one could receive the 'Baptism with the Holy Spirit.' The final stage of our redemption will also come at a precise moment in history

Christians joyfully await the objective return and appearing of Yeshua. This will be the objective fulfillment in history of the Feast of Tabernacles Eager believers however, are not just passively waiting for, or speculating about this great event but are actively preparing themselves for the final state of redemption that will be made available at that time.

Tabernacles anticipates the return of the Lord and the 'Marriage Supper of the Lamb' (Rev. 19:9) *"Alleluia! For the Lord God Omnipotent reigns! Let us be glad and rejoice and give Him glory, for the marriage of the Lamb has come and His wife has made herself ready. And to her it was granted to be arrayed in fine linen, clean and bright, for the fine linen is the righteous acts of the saints. Then he said*

105

to me, *"Write: Blessed are those who are called to the marriage supper of the Lamb!"'* (Rev. 19:6-9)

As we wait for the return of the Lord and the historic fulfillment of the Feast of Tabernacles we should not be distracted with speculation about the future but prepare ourselves through holy living and 'righteous deeds.' Paul wrote that the goal of life was *"to know Him in the power of His resurrection and the fellowship of His sufferings becoming like Him in death that if possible I may attain to the resurrection from the dead. Not that I have already obtained this or am already perfect ... but one thing I do forgetting what lies behind and straining forward to what lies ahead I press on toward the goal for the prize of the upward call of God in Christ Jesus."* (Phil. 3:10-14)

Peter says that we are guarded by God's power through faith for *"a salvation ready to be revealed in the last time"* (1 Peter 1: 15) Since his readers had already experienced both the Passover and the Pentecost dimension of their salvation he is referring here to the final stage of our salvation

106

which will break forth in the last days. Then immortality and glory will be experienced by the expectant Church. All who have entered the Passover and Pentecost dimension of salvation should eagerly prepare for Tabernacles.

Just as the generation that was alive at the time of Jesus was the first to receive the new birth and the Baptism with the Holy Spirit so the generation that witnesses the return of Jesus will be the first to receive the fullness of redemption.

Zechariah foretold a day when the remnant of the nations would come up to Jerusalem every year to worship the King. "*And it shall come to pass that everyone who is left of all the nations which came against Jerusalem, shall go up from -year to year to worship the King, the Lord of hosts, and to keep the Feast of Tabernacles.*" (Zech. 14:16) Before Messiah Jesus returns all the nations will come against Jerusalem, but the survivors will come and acknowledge the King in Jerusalem.

Tabernacles anticipates the return and triumphant enthronement of the Lord in Jerusalem, and the establishment of His rule over all the nations. There can be no fulfillment of Feast of Tabernacles without the return and enthronement of the Messiah. According to scriptures all the Feasts had to be *celebrated "in the place where God would choose."* (Leviticus 23:24) We know that this place was Jerusalem. The place where the Feasts were celebrated throughout the Temple period was Jerusalem. Likewise the only place where these Feasts could be fulfilled by Jesus is Jerusalem. Only in Jerusalem can the Feasts be fulfilled. This is why all eyes are on Jerusalem again as Messiah Jesus prepares to fulfill this Feast of Tabernacles. Let our hearts and prayers be there also as we say: " Come Lord Jesus!"

A Foretaste Of Tabernacles Today

As we wait for the unfoldment of God's glorious plan, we can today walk in foretastes of the union with God which the Feast of Tabernacles symbolizes. Jesus prayed that we would 'all be one' even as He was one with His Father, and that His 'glory' would be also seen in us. (Jn 17:20-26)

As we await the final consummation of our redemption we are called to walk in total union with the Lord today. When we walk in union with God, and love Him and obey Him with all our hearts. He puts more and more of His glory on us. (See John 17) This is a foretaste of The Feast of Tabernacles when God's people will walk in the continual glory of God. When God's people truly walk in love they have a foretaste of the Feast of fullness.

"For this reason I bow my knees before the Father, from whom every family in heaven and on earth is named, that according to the riches of his glory he may grant you to be strengthened with might through his Spirit in the inner man, and that Christ may dwell in your hearts through faith; that you, being rooted and grounded in love, may have power to comprehend with all the saints what is the

breadth and length and height and depth, and to know the love of Christ which surpasses knowledge, that you may be filled with all the fullness of God. Now to him who by the power at work within us is able to do far more abundantly than all that we ask or think, to him be glory in the church and in Christ Jesus to all generations, for ever and ever. Amen. (Ephesians 3: 14-21)

Chapter 8

THE FEASTS OF PURIM & DEDICATION

The feasts of Purim[3] and Hanukkah[4] or Dedication were not given as part of the Sinai Law, but were added much later. They do not carry the same prophetic significance as the Feasts given on Mount Sinai. Nevertheless in the sovereignty of God they were added to commemorate and celebrate two decisive events in the History of Israel.

Both Feasts recall events that have to do with the survival of the Israeli people. Purim commemorates their survival of attempted genocide and Hanukkah celebrates an effort through

---

[3] The word "Purim" means "lots"

[4] The word "Hanukkah" means "dedication"

persecution to destroy their worship and faith. These feasts were added because God wants the vulnerability of the people of Israel to persecution and their ultimate survival to be constantly remembered by them and by believers of all generations,

The Feast of Purim (Lots)

The Feast of Purim recalls the events of the Book of Esther. It commemorates the survival of the Jewish people in their days of exile in Babylon at a time when the Medes controlled Babylon. Haman, the Prime Minister of Babylon devised a plan to exterminate and annihilate the Jewish people. The plan was overturned by the bravery of Esther who was married to Ahasureus the King of the Medes and her cousin Mordechai who risked their lives for the survival of their people. There was a sudden reversal of fortunes for the Jewish people and the genocide was averted. The events take place around

563 B.C. The Feast is celebrated on the 14th and 15th of Adar[5] each year.

An annual celebration of the events of their survival was decreed and commanded for the people of Israel.

Purim & The Crucifixion Of Jesus

Purim recalls that the gallows that Haman built to kill, Mordechai the champion of the Jewish people, turned into his own gallows.

What a picture of the crucifixion of Jesus who was crucified on Calvary! His cross did not destroy Him but destroyed the authority of the devil over the human race. The Devil, seeking to destroy Jesus actually brought destruction down upon Him.

The cross, the gallows that the devil so cleverly designed to destroy God's Son, became the means of the devils own destruction. Jesus over come hatred with forgiveness and God the Father overcame death and destruction with resurrection.

---

[5] Adar roughly corresponds to the western month of March.

"He disarmed the principalities and powers and made a public example of them, triumphing over them in him." (Colossians 2:15)

On his cross Jesus destroyed the devils right of accusation over all humans because he took the judgment we all deserve. He, being innocent could not be held by death and we are forgiven and released from Satan's dominion through Him. In seeking to destroy Jesus' authority Satan, like Haman, destroyed His own.

Purim & Anti Semitism

The annual commemoration of these events is God's way of reminding us that the spirits that motivated Haman to come against the Jews are with us to the end of the age. These evil spirits hate the Jewish people because of the purposes of God that are to being worked out through them.

Again and again through history even in Christian countries these evil spirits and attitudes have risen against the Jews. Most tragic of all revivals of the spirit of Haman was the rise of Hitler and the Holocaust of over 6,000,000 Jews that

GOOD NEWS IN ISRAEL'S FEASTS

followed his actions. In the days of Hitler unfortunately there were too few Esthers and Mordechais who spoke up in defense of the Jews. Because of ignorance of God's eternal plan for the Jewish people Christians have often abetted their political leaders when they persecuted the Jewish people.

Even today evil spirits rise with insane propaganda against the Jewish people and the state of Israel. In these days the spirit is active through fanatical Islam which seeks to destroy Jewish presence in Israel. Biblically illiterate Christians who have never learned the lesson of Purim often assist them in their efforts. The spirits that motivated Haman while they can never succeed will always try their utmost to destroy God 's People.

If the lesson of Purim had been preserved among believers the conditions that created the Holocaust would never have happened.

Today the foul spirit of murderous anti Semitism is active in much of the Islamic world, Will believers remain passive as Israel suffers onslaught after onslaught of wars and suicide killing directed at their destruction? As we study Purim let us learn the lesson that believers should remember that the people of Israel are especially vulnerable to persecution. They will always need the forthright voices of friends in high places like Esther and of vigilant watchmen like Mordechai.

The book of Zechariah shows us that in the last days the spirit of Anti-Semitism will arise among the nations. All the nations will come against Israel, but that God will oppose them. At that time the Messiah (Jesus) will return to this earth and His feet will stand on the Mount of Olives. (Zechariah Chapter 14)

"Then the LORD will go forth and fight against those nations as when he fights on a day of battle. On that day his feet shall stand on the Mount of Olives which lies before Jerusalem on the east; and the Mount of Olives shall be split in two from east to west by a very wide valley; so that one half of the Mount shall withdraw northward, and the other half southward." (Zechariah 14:3-4)

From this it appears that the Spirit of Haman will eventually come against Israel one final time in an attempt to divide Jerusalem. This item they conflict will be ended not by the intervention of Mordechai but by the intervention Of Jesus Himself.

God warned the nations that He would bless the nations that bless Israel and curse those nations that oppose Israel. (Genesis 12:3) Blessing the Jewish people brings a blessing on our nations. Anti-Semitism and anti-Zionism brings a curse on our nations.

This principle is part of His everlasting Covenant with Abraham and His descendants through Isaac and Jacob. Believers in Jesus from the gentiles are grafted into the commonwealth of Israel. We should separate

> *Believers should separate ourselves from the thought forms of the nations, put on the mind of Christ and stand in faith to see God's purpose for Israel fulfilled.*

117

ourselves from the thought forms of the nations, put on the mind of Christ and stand in faith to see God's purpose for Israel fulfilled.

Many will be called, like Mordechai and Esther of old, to speak up in public and in print for Israel. Our churches should teach their people the responsibility to pray for Israel. Though Israel may frequently disobey God, He has called them to a destiny in their land not only for their own sakes but also for the sake of the whole world. (See Romans chapter 11)

Many of the world's statesmen have been educated in churches. They have been taught that anti Semitism is a crime against humanity, but they have not been instructed about God's eternal purposes for the people of Israel. They have not been taught the Biblical message that the Lord has assigned the Land if Israel to them as an "everlasting possession".

Because of this ignorance many Christian-educated statesmen are even in these days involved in efforts that support those determined to destroy the State of Israel. This brings a great stain on our lands.

Purim & The End Of The Age

Purim also recalls that at Purim the God of Israel removed His enemies and the ten sons of Haman were defeated and killed.

Soon the God of creation and redemption will put an end to the nations and systems that oppose the rule of the Messiah and the people of the Messiah - the Jews and the Christians. In that day the Kingdom's of this world will become *"the kingdoms of our Lord and of His Christ; and he shall reign for ever and ever."* (Revelation 11:15) Many antichrists have come and gone and eventually like the ten sons of Haman they will all be defeated.

To remember Purim is to remember that God's plan for the Jewish people and for the church can never be defeated. Eventually tyrannical leaders will all fall and God will spread His loving peace over the whole earth. However, God's victory requires our obedience, cooperation and willingness

119

to lay our lives on the line like Esther and to speak up and act like Mordechai.

God's ultimate victory is sure. The only question is whose side will we be on - on the side of the Lord's purposes or on the side of those who fight against God's will.

The Feast of Dedication
The Story behind The Feast

In the days of the Macabees about 169 years before the birth of Christ the Feast of Dedication known in Hebrew as Chanukah was added to the Jewish calendar.

In 169 B.C. Antiochus Epihanes the Hellenized ruler of Syria was defeated in a campaign against Israel. Returning in defeat he passed through Jerusalem, destroyed much of the city and slaughtered many of the inhabitants. He desecrated the Temple and stole its treasures. To show his contempt for the God of Israel and of everything the Jews held dear he sacrificed a pig to Jupiter in the Holy Temple, and forbade the observance of the Jewish Feasts and rites.

Matthias the leader of the priestly Macabee family and his four sons including Judas led a revolt against these outrages. They succeeded, through guerilla tactics, in expelling the Syrians and on Kislev 25th (Kislev roughly corresponds to December) they reconsecrated the Temple and erected a new altar to the Lord in Jerusalem.

They relit the perpetual light of the Temple but found only enough consecrated oil to last one day. Miraculously the little cruse of oil lasted for eight days until a new supply of consecrated oil was prepared.

The Macabees decreed that a special feast lasting eight days (like the cruse of oil) should be held forever to celebrate the dedication of the Temple and the restoration of true worship.

Because of the miracle of the cruse of oil it is also a Festival of Lights. Special Hanukkah lamps are lit with nine lamps. One light is distinguished from the others and is know as the "servant light". The servant light recalls the cruse of oil that should

121

only have been sufficient for one day yet was able to provide light for eight days.

The Feast of Dedication in the Ministry of Jesus

During His lifetime Jesus naturally celebrated the Feast of Hanukkah each year. It was a festal time in the middle of Winter.

John recalls Jesus' last Hanukkah in Jerusalem. Jerusalem was astir with the debate as to whether Jesus was or was not the Messiah. " *We must work the works of him who sent me, while it is day; night comes, when no one can work. As long as I am in the world, I am the light of the world. ….. I am the door; if any one enters by me, he will be saved, and will go in and out and find pasture. The thief comes only to steal and kill and destroy; I came that they may have life, and have it abundantly. I am the good shepherd[6]. The good shepherd lays down his life for the sheep. ….*

*It was the **feast of the Dedication** at Jerusalem; it was winter, and Jesus was walking in*

---

[6] 'Good Shepherd' is a clear Messianic Title (Psalm 80:1)

the temple, in the portico of Solomon. So the Jews gathered round him and said to him, "How long will you keep us in suspense? If you are the Christ, tell us plainly." Jesus answered them, "I told you, and you do not believe. The works that I do in my Father's name, they bear witness to me; but you do not believe, because you do not belong to my sheep. My sheep hear my voice, and I know them, and they follow me; and I give them eternal life, and they shall never perish, and no one shall snatch them out of my hand. My Father, who has given them to me, is greater than all, and no one is able to snatch them out of the Father's hand. I and the Father are one." (John 9: 4-5; 10:9-11, 23-30)

One of the most critical moments of Jesus' ministry took place during the Feast of Dedication. It was during this Feast that He declared openly that He is "the light of the world" and "The Good Shepherd" (a synonym for the Messiah). He then declared that the works that the Father did through Him testified that He was indeed the Messiah.

The Feast of Dedication then was the day when Jesus *definitively* and *openly* proclaimed to Israel that He was and is the Messiah. Dedication could therefore be also called Messiah Day or Christ day.

It is interesting that on the 25th day of the western month December (that corresponds most closely to the Hebrew month of Chislev) Christians celebrate Messiah Day or Christmas

Many trace present day Christmas to the Emperor Constantine, who merged Christian tradition with pagan festivals. Though many pagan, secular and customs have crept into the celebration of Christmas it is still the day that corresponds to Jesus proclamation that He was the Messiah. Because materialistic elements threaten to submerge its real meaning, is no reason for believers not to celebrate Messiah Day or Christmas. If we keep the Hebrew Calendar we can celebrate it on the 25th of Kislev or if we keep the Western calendar we can celebrate the 25th of December. As we celebrate

Dedication[7] and Christmas we should enter into the reality behind the feast. Believers can make this a time of

- remembering God's eternal plan for Jerusalem, which the pagans of the day tried to obliterate
- rededication of the temple of our own bodies to God's purposes by presenting our bodies anew to be living sacrifices available for the Lord's agenda and loosed from selfish living (See Romans 12:1-2)
- Celebrate the fact that Jesus the babe of Bethlehem, and the great teacher and healer is also the Messiah, who has freed us from sin and the powers of darkness.
-

According to the writings of Paul believers, are not required to keep the ritual of Feasts but we should concentrate on understanding and obeying the message behind each Feast. On the other hand

---

[7] The only biblical reference to the Feast of Dedication (apart from the apocrypha) is in the New Testament

because we are not *required* to keep the ritual of feast does not mean that we may not celebrate feasts and use them to remember the great realities of our redemption. They are powerful pedagogic devices to implant the message and the reality of God's redemptive work in our minds and consciousness

If the cleansing of the Temple in the days of the Macabees marks a decisive moment in history how much more can believers celebrate the coming of Jesus.

Today it is commonly known that Jesus was not born during the month of December, however the 25th of Chislev is the day He proclaimed He was the Christ. Therefore 25th of Chislev, though it is not Jesus' birthday, it is indeed Christ day. Constantine got it right for all the wrong reasons!

Remember Zion

How sad it would be today if we celebrate Chanukah and fail to remember the eternal purposes of God for Jerusalem. This is especially relevant at this time when the nations once again seek to tear away the temple area from the people of Israel as in the days of the Macabees. It was probably for this reason, realizing that the forces of darkness would always oppose the plan of God for the Jewish people's return to their land and to their city that God permitted this feast to be established as an eternal observance.

Zechariah tells us that at the end of the age the nations will once again divide Jerusalem, but the Lord will oppose and 'fight against' those nations that seek to divide Jerusalem" (See Zechariah 14)

It would be equally tragic to celebrate the dedication of the Temple in Jerusalem in 169 BC and fail to dedicate the temple of our own bodies to the Lord. The defilement of the world - its ways its thoughts and its values are ever seeking to extinguish the light in our lives. We must constantly eject thoughts and attitudes that are defiling and out of harmony with the word and ways of God.

"I beseech you therefore, brethren, by the mercies of God, that ye present your bodies a living sacrifice, holy, acceptable unto God, which is your reasonable service. And be not conformed to this

world: but be ye transformed by the renewing of your mind, that ye may prove what is that good, and acceptable, and perfect, will of God." (Romans 12:1-2)

When we come to God through Jesus we should present our bodies to Him. This is the way we serve Him. Our primary dedication should not be to career or the other agendas of self or of this world but to live for the advancement of God's kingdom and mercy in the world. Have you dedicated your temple your body and it's energies to be a vessel for God to use to bless Him and the world we live in?

It would be equally tragic to celebrate Christmas and fail to allow the Messiah His rightful place in our hearts. As He comes into our hearts He cleanses the Temple of our lives and makes our lives a center of His light and hope.

If we keep these festivals let us be sure to touch the meaning and the reality behind them festivals.

CHAPTER 9

THE SABBATH

Interwoven with the seven Feasts of the Lord given to Moses is the Sabbath

"Say to the people of Israel, The appointed feasts of the LORD which you shall proclaim as holy convocations, my appointed feasts, are these. Six days shall work be done; but on the seventh day is a Sabbath of solemn rest, a holy convocation; you shall do no work; it is a Sabbath to the LORD in all your dwellings." (Leviticus 23: 2-3)

"Remember the sabbath day, to keep it holy. Six days you shall labor, and do all your work; but the seventh day is a sabbath to the LORD your God; in it you shall not do any work, you, or your son, or

your daughter, your manservant, or your maidservant, or your cattle, or the sojourner who is within your gates; for in six days the LORD made heaven and earth, the sea, and all that is in them, and rested the seventh day; therefore the LORD blessed the sabbath day and hallowed it." (Ex 20:8-11)

The Sabbath is a mini festival held every week. It sums up the message of all the Feasts it is a time of celebration of the Lord's goodness and faithfulness and a time to remember that all our blessings come from Him.

The Sabbath is a reminder to all that we live from the goodness and provision of God our Creator and Keeper. He who made us is also He who keeps us. We do not live from our work but from His blessing. Work is important and six days are to be devoted to work and one to rest. The rest reminds us that we are not slaves. We live not from our work but from God. Work is part of the means of provision. God provides us with the talents the energy and the gifts to do our work, but it is His blessing that enriches us. So the Sabbath shows two elements blessing and work. Work without blessing is slavery.

The Sabbath was given before the law and it is a reminder that we are made for fellowship with God to enjoy His blessing all our days.

Life without time for rest, relaxation and fellowship with God is slavery. We become driven by events rather than guided by God. Work has an addictive pressure that if not checked with rest can drive us from the presence of God.

Isaiah says *"For thus says the Lord GOD, the Holy One of Israel; in returning and rest shall you be saved; in quietness and in confidence shall be your strength: and you would not.* (Isa 30:15)

Jesus said, *"The Sabbath was made for man, not man for the Sabbath."* (Matt. 2:27) Legalistic observance of Sabbath is not the issue. The issue is do we stop to recall the goodness of God and rejoice in His provision of life and of redemption.' The Sabbath is a gift of God to us for our rest and replenishment physically, mentally and spiritually. Medical science confirms the extraordinary benefits

131

to be received from ceasing from activity on a weekly basis

The most important ingredient of Sabbath is to cease from work and to remember the Lord's reality,

> *A life of forgetfulness of God's mercy, goodness and our dependence on Him is doomed to frustration, futility and lack of creativity.*

blessings and goodness. A life of forgetfulness of God's mercy, goodness and our dependence on Him is doomed to frustration, futility and lack of creativity. God gave us the Sabbath not only to remember Him but also to be a time of refreshment

The Rest Of Faith

"Therefore, while the promise of entering his rest remains, let us fear lest any of you be judged to have failed to reach it. For good news came to us just as to them; but the message which they heard did not benefit them, because it did not meet with faith in the hearers. For we who have believed enter that rest, as he has said, "As I swore in my wrath, 'They shall never enter my rest,'" although his

works were finished from the foundation of the world. For he has somewhere spoken of the seventh day in this way, "And God rested on the seventh day from all his works." And again in this place he said, "They shall never enter my rest." Since therefore it remains for some to enter it, and those who formerly received the good news failed to enter because of disobedience, again he sets a certain day, "Today," saying through David so long afterward, in the words already quoted, "Today, when you hear his voice, do not harden your hearts." For if Joshua had given them rest, God would not speak later of another day. So then, there remains a Sabbath rest for the people of God; for whoever enters God's rest also ceases from his labors as God did from his. Let us therefore strive to enter that rest, that no one fall by the same sort of disobedience." (Hebrews 4:1-11)

Here we are given insight into the real rest of the believer. The rest of those who know their sins are forgiven The rest of those who know they are reconciled to God through Jesus Christ and the rest

133

of knowing we are in covenant relationship with the God who supplies our need according to His riches in glory in Christ Jesus.

The issue of Sabbath is the issue of the rest of faith, not the issue of the rituals of observance.

Many are confused about which day of the week should be observed as the Sabbath and how strict our observance should be. Should there be one day set aside as our day of rest? and which day should it be should it be - the Hebrew Sabbath or the Western Sunday?

The real issue is have we entered into the rest of faith? Do we really know that we are reconciled to God through the finished work of Jesus on the cross? Do we take time to rest, thank God and remember His benefits? Do we take time to love Him, seek His blessings and direction. such time is more important than our time of work? Without a Sabbath rest we destroy the goose that lays the golden egg, by not nurturing our relationship with God who provides us with everything we have, and by not replenishing our minds and bodies. Without Sabbath rest we fall back into slavery always working and never enjoying its fruits. The *"cares of this world, the deceitfulness of riches choke the word"* and our fruitfulness in the Kingdom. (Mark 13:22)

Many who are most strict in their observance miss the point that it is not the day but resting in faith in the goodness of God that is the important thing. He is with us always and we have found refuge in Him. Taking time to realize who sustains us, who supplies our need, who supplies our health, and our opportunities in life is the essence of the Sabbath observance. We can rest in the stability of God's commitment to us and renew our dependence on Him.

Which Day Should We Observe?

Surprisingly, the Bible does not specify which day should be observed but that every seventh[8] day should be a day of rest. Christians put

---

[8] This may surprise many but it is a fact. Sabbath means rest. The Bible specifies that one day one week should be a day of rest, every seventh day should be a day of rest. It does not specify where you start counting.

it at the first day of the week remembering the resurrection and Jews as the end of the week remembering the creation. The Christian day of rest celebrates the rest provided for us by the finished work of the cross. Rest is not only for restoration and refreshment but also for ceasing of activity.

The idea of giving God the first fruits offering of our week is appealing as Paul says: *"if the first fruits is holy the whole lump is holy."* (Romans 11:16) Giving the Lord the first day in rest and thanksgiving and remembrance causes His blessing to be released in greater measure on the rest of the week.

Many advocate Christians should return to the Jewish calendar but the early Christians (all Jews) did not impose this on the nations to which the were scattered. What they did share was the principle of rest. The main ingredients of rest are ceasing from work, acknowledging God's blessing and remembering His goodness.

"One man esteems one day as better than another, while another man esteems all days alike.

Let every one be fully convinced in his own mind. He who observes the day, observes it in honor of the Lord. He also who eats, eats in honor of the Lord, since he gives thanks to God; while he who abstains, abstains in honor of the Lord and gives thanks to God. None of us lives to himself, and none of us dies to himself." (Romans 14: 5-7)

Paul recognizes that people have different convictions on the issue of Sabbath observance. He desires that we respect each other's convictions. Some people have more scruples than others about the details and specific day of observance. Those who have greater liberty should not despise them and they should not despise those with greater liberty. The important thing is to realize our salvation depends on the finished work of the Cross, and that we enter into rest on this issue, and not in the details of our Sabbath observance or the day we choose to rest..

What a gift the rest of the Lord is to His people especially to those who enter the rest of faith and rejoice in God's faithful eternal, mercy and goodness.

"Near restful waters He leads me to revive my drooping spirit,

Surely goodness and mercy will follow me all the days of my life and I will dwell in the house of the house of the Lord forever." (Psalm 23)

"Be still, and know that I am God: I will be exalted among the heathen, I will be exalted in the earth." (Ps 46:10) This is the essence of Sabbath.

CHAPTER 8

SUMMARY & CONCLUSION

The Feasts of the Lord provide us with a perfect type and pre-figuring of the stages of redemption in the Life of a New Testament believer. In Leviticus 23:2 God says: *"The feasts of the Lord which you shall proclaim are holy convocations"*

The word "feasts" could also be translated as "appointments" and the word "convocations" can also be translated as "rehearsals".

The Levitical Feasts are not just remembrances of past events but are seven rehearsals for God's appointments with man in history. They are also rehearsals for the major

139

appointments with God to which He invites each one of us.

Too often in the church we have made a plateau of one of these appointments, the appointment of the New Birth for example or the appointment with Baptism with the Holy Spirit. The time has come however, to meet God in all His appointments with us and to prepare for the major appointment which still awaits us at the end of this age.

The Body of Christ on the earth today is being summoned to prepare to be led into fuller realms of victory and union with God. At the right time the final appointment and dimension of redemption that is anticipated by the Feast of Tabernacles will be revealed. *"When He appears we shall be like Him, for we shall see Him as He is."* (1 John 3:2)

No generation of Christians has yet attained to the full glory that is our hope and goal. In our day the Lord is preparing His people, by bringing us through the various stages of redemption prefigured in the Jewish feasts, so that we may be ready for the glory that is coming to us at the time of His appearing. Therefore, it is vitally important that none of us get stagnated in our Christian walk, but that we continue to press on towards the high call of life in Christ Jesus.

The new birth is only a beginning; Pentecost, or the Baptism with the Holy Spirit, is not the end. God is summoning us to a greater closeness to Himself, to holiness and to prepare for the glory that is soon to be revealed. The hour is upon us! Have you heard the trumpet summoning you to a further depth in God? Don't stop at Pentecost. There is more. Do not be surprised as the refining process (Atonement) is intensified to put sin out of our lives and get us ready for the HOUR OF GLORY! We are being prepared! (See Exodus 23, Leviticus 23, Deut. 16, 1 Cor 15, Rom. 8)

As we wait for this hour let us remember that *"He who has this hope purifies himself."*

> The Holy Spirit is preparing us for the return of the Lord and the completion redemption

141

(1 Jn. 3:3) This purification brings us to an ever increasing union with Jesus (the union spoken of in John Chapter 17) even as we await the fulfillment of the Feast of Tabernacles. Transfiguration and union begin NOW for those who are willing, and will be completed at the hour of His appearing.

So we see the Feasts of the Lord provide us with a perfect type and pre-figuring of the appointments of redemption in the life of a New Testament believer. Let's enter into the reality prefigured by each of the Feast. Let us not stop at any until all is fulfilled.

The Christian faith is not only a faith but it is also a "blessed hope." Faith builds on the foundation of the finished work of Yeshua; hope catches a vision of the greater glory that is yet to be revealed. At the right time this final stage of redemption that is anticipated by the Feast of Tabernacles will be completed in Jerusalem, when Jesus' feet shall stand on the Mount of Olives and He reigns from the throne of David in the "City of the Great King." (Zechariah 14:1-4; Acts 1:11)

142

PRAYER

Father, I am in awe of Your plan of redemption. Complete what You have begun in me as I present myself to You to be changed 'from glory to glory'. Keep me blameless in spirit and soul and body until your appearing.

Thank you that through *Passover* You have covered my sins. Through *Unleavened Bread* You have removed them and set me free. Through *First Fruits* you have given me New Life. Through *Pentecost* you have anointed me to be your witness.

Through Trumpets cause me to awaken to the signs of the times and to recognize Your unfolding plan, for your church and for Israel. Through Atonement I release on my Scapegoat, Jesus, all my guilt, grief, rejection, sorrow, pain and sickness and I submit to Your refining processes. Through Tabernacles let me respond to Your call to ever-increasing union and love for You and fill me with living hope as I await Your return and the completion of redemption.

143

144

Books by Paul & Nuala Higgins

Christianity Without Religion

This book presents Christianity not as a religion, but as an exciting relationship with our Creator and Redeemer. The O'Higgins unwrap its truths from the cobwebs of tradition to unveil the exciting message of the gospel in a way that makes it good news again.
(200 pages)

"Have You Received the Holy Spirit"

This mini-book clearly explains the relationship between the New Birth and the Baptism of The Holy Spirit and why every believer should have these two realties in their lives. It is a practical teaching showing how to receive. We encourage you to get it in bulk as a tool of evangelism.

The Tree Of Life

This is a book of insight on the importance of living in the realm of trust and faith. It gives fresh insight to equip the believer to forgive, and live free of regrets. It is an important revelation for living in freedom and love in the kingdom of God and to find healing from life's hurts.
(68 pages)

The One New Man Series

This series is designed to create a greater understanding of the Gospel in the light of our Hebrew roots and to providing a greater awareness into the vital connection between Jews and Christians and to understanding Christianity in the light of the Old Testament (Tanak)

The Four Covenants

This is the first in the "One  New Man Series". It explains the plan of God for the redemption of the world in the light of the major covenants He made with Israel. It is a clear explanation of the four major covenants and the relationship of the New Covenant with the earlier covenants God made with Israel. (64 pages)

New Testament Believers & The Law

 This is the Second in the 'One New Man Series'. It tackles the controversial issue of believers relationship with the Old Testament Law, in a way that both clarifies the areas of evangelical liberty and respecting the eternal purpose of the law. An important issue in today's' church is clearly explained by the O'Higgins in this book. (88 pages)

"Good News In Israel's Feasts"

 This is one of the best books available on the feasts, the O'Higgins give remarkable insight into the relationship between the Feasts of The Lord and the believer's full salvation. They take the Feasts from the realm of ritual into practical realties for all believers today. (120 pages)

To order these books write to Reconciliation Outreach, P.O. Box 2778, Stuart, FL 34995, USA Tel. 1-800-258 5416 or 1-772-283-6920

ABOUT THE AUTHORS

Paul & Nuala O'Higgins are the directors of Reconciliation Outreach. They are natives of Ireland now living in Stuart, Florida. They travel extensively in an international ministry of teaching and reconciliation. They are dedicated to worldwide interdenominational evangelism. Paul holds a doctorate in Biblical theology. They are the authors of several books and are called to be part of the movement to renew restore and prepare the church end of age.

Dear Reader,

This book and our other books are written for your edification, exhortation and comfort and for God's glory. If they are a blessing to you tell others, and make sure your Christian bookstore has these books on hand. We welcome your comments, and would love to hear from you.

In His great love and service,
Paul & Nuala